In Search of a Meaningful Life

A Guide to Finding the Purpose of Life and Exploring the Possibilities to Fulfill It

Bibhuti Mazumder, Ph.D.

Noble House
Baltimore, Maryland

In Search of a Meaningful Life
A Guide to Finding the Purpose of Life and Exploring the Possibilities to Fulfill It

Library of Congress
Cataloging in Publication Data
ISBN 1-56167-415-X

Library of Congress Card Catalog Number:
97-076328

Published by

8019 Belair Road, Suite 10
Baltimore, Maryland 21236

Manufactured in the United States of America

This book
is dedicated with
profound love and great
compassion to those who are searching
for a deeper understanding
of the hidden purpose
of life and the essence
of a joyful coexistence
with all beings.

Acknowledgments

This book is an expression of the ideas drawn from many sources. Most of the quotations are taken from the New Testament published by Gideons International, the Gita, and the Upanishads. It gives me great pleasure to take this opportunity to acknowledge and express my deepest appreciation to people who have assisted and inspired me from the beginning to the end by their constant enthusiastic encouragement and constructive criticism.

Innumerable discussions with my son, Dr. Amitabha Mazumder, have profoundly influenced me to express the message I wanted to convey. I am deeply indebted to him for the way the book has taken shape.

I am greatly thankful to my beloved niece, Miss Indira Debchoudhury, for typing the manuscript with great care.

I am also thankful to Kimberly Barker and the staff at noble House for their assitance.

Most of all I am eternally grateful to my wife, Nilima Mazumder, who by her dedication and expanded vision made the manuscript worthy of publication. Without her support I could not have finished the book. She is my greatest blessing in all my endeavors.

Introduction

Every human being has a unique talent for what he or she is supposed to become and do here on earth. Only he or she can do the job assigned to him or her. Life becomes satisfying to the extent that this purpose is fulfilled. Without the awareness of who we are and where we need to go to find the purpose of being here, life becomes a big puzzle—the missing pieces of which would remain forever shrouded in mystery. A meaningful life dawns with the quest of the hidden purpose of life and exploring the possibilities to fulfill it.

Life is not meant to be a sequence of pains and sufferings, but an abundance of joy and laughter. This joy, this delight, can be realized only when the life is based on a spiritual foundation. True spirituality as portrayed in this book is not far removed from the earthly life. It is not an escape from the world we live in, but a way to reach the inner power and face the challenges of life. It gives you courage and strength to solve day-to-day problems of family and professional life, control the mind, reduce tension, and resist the temptations of modern society. It blossoms in the discharge of the smallest activities of every day life and takes you back to the essence of being human when you drift away from it.

The degradation of our society today stems mainly from the lack of awareness of what is within us. Being ignorant of our true nature we seek external solutions to problems rooted within. In our search for security and prosperity we have abandoned ourselves and are constantly drifting away from human values and virtues. Not by legislation but by the change in the way of living we can stop this drifting to the degree that we align ourselves with the inner Divinity and let our true nature manifest in our every day life.

If you think that things are not working the way they should and you are just drifting aimlessly through life, that is a clear indication that you should shift the center of consciousness and get in touch with your inner power. This book is written with the deepest concern for the pains and problems of life. It will provide guidance to awaken you to the innermost truth of your being where pains and problems cease to exist.

Follow the spiritual path paved right here
And become one with every being,
Discover the relationship of God and humanity
To experience the delight of living.

The first chapter, "Getting Ready for a New Beginning," tells us that there is a divine center within us which is our natural state—our real Self—and is the source of infinite power, knowledge, and bliss. When you align yourself with your natural state, the inner power begins to respond in a mysterious way to what you need to change yourself to bolster self-confidence and straighten out priorities of life.

The second chapter "Alter the Pattern of Your Thinking," explains that you are what you are thinking all the time. Thoughts are born in the depths of the mind. By controlling the mind the destructive and selfish thoughts can be filtered out and replaced by thoughts that are noble, kind, and loving. Desire, wrath, and greed are the obstacles to growth that lead to the ruin of the soul. This chapter gives clues to control these feelings and emotions and move freely amidst the world of passion. Happiness is a by-product of this endeavor to forsake pride, wrath, and greed and reach the deepest wisdom of human consciousness.

The third chapter, "Love and Serve All Beings," says that love is the essence of existence and a potent transformative force that brings joy where there is sorrow and happiness, where there is pain. The eternal flow of love is sustained by the noble acts of giving, serving and forgiving. All life is giving. The more you give the more you grow to become a better human being. True giving is non-egotistic and is free from the desire of name and fame. It is distinguished by the marks of love, unselfishness and humility. Service to humanity is the best way to worship God who resides in the heart of all beings. We progress on the path of selfless service by increasing our awareness of the sorrows and pains of others and honestly looking for a solution within ourselves. Forgiveness is the sign of growth and compassion that brings joy and laughter to life. The moment we forgive we realize that we are not separate and are connected by the same cord of love. Negative thoughts of bitterness and resentment are then released and the mind is transformed to heal the breaches in relationship.

The fourth chapter is "Pay Attention and Live the Present." To pay attention means total oneness with what you are doing, seeing, hearing, or feeling now. This is the most natural way to experience life fully, relieve pain, and achieve a worthwhile life. To live the present is to merge completely with what is happening at this moment without any distraction. It brings harmony between the inner and outer actualities of life and reveals the extraordinary in most ordinary happenings of everyday life. We can develop and intensify our ability to merge completely with the happenings of the moment in four ways, depending on the tendencies of the mind. These ways are called yogas. Yogas are very powerful methods for inner transformation, growth and self-discovery. In all these yogas the mind attains one-pointed awareness focused only on the present, since in this awareness there is neither past nor future. There is no longer the dualism of the subject and the object, the knower and the known.

The last chapter is "Live Your Religion and Take Refuge in God." Religion is not contemplation on an abstract and conceptual being living in a far off land up above the sky, in the midst of distant stars. Religion is the guide for the development of human consciousness to experience the universe just as it is. Religion offers a splendid opportunity to realize the interconnection and oneness of all things and beings. To live the religion means to experience the highest level of human thought that goes beyond personal pleasure, profit or loss, success or failure to a greater dimension of love, service, and sacrifice. We can reach the higher level of consciousness by converting the work we do for living into worship. Work becomes worship when we rise above our normal consciousness into another level of awareness where personal ego and selfish desire do not exist. Prayer is the best means to uplift our consciousness from the imprisonment of personal gratification to the oneness and union with all beings. Prayer consecrates all our actions, removes ignorance, and leads us to an expanded vision of who we really are and feel the richness of life.

Don't miss the opportunity
To be useful to others,
Others will then become
Your own brothers and sisters.

Bibhuti Mazumder, Ph.D.
July 1997
Baltimore

Table of Contents

> Awake, sleep no more
> It is time for a new beginning
> By the awareness of the present
> Know the truth of your being.

I

Getting Ready for a New Beginning

"I am the light of the world.
He that followeth me
Shall not walk in darkness:
But shall have the light of life."
St. John 8:12

God—The spirit of existences
    Is in the depth of your soul
Change yourself to go within
    And bring the world under your control.
Our outward happenings
    Originate in the Spirit's power
That shapes our lives
    And allows miracles to occur.
Stay on spiritual course
    All through the darkest night
Ignorance will vanish
    By the glow of the divine light.
Pains and sufferings
    Are God's mysterious device.
To let us grow
    And overcome vice.
With patience and firm determination
    Begin the spiritual journey
You will end up in happiness
    Peace and harmony.

"God is light
And in Him is no darkness at all."
1 John 1:5

In Quest of Hidden Power

A retrospective survey of our lives reveals that the most significant happenings that shaped our lives are not fully the outcome of our own planning. Life seems to be the play of some hidden power that operates behind everything we do and directs the course of our destiny. It makes life an ongoing eternal process of evolution and takes humanity into higher levels of consciousness.

In this power lies the blue print of the unique talent that each one of us has for what we are suppose to do here on earth. Life becomes satisfying to the extent to which this purpose is fulfilled. The awareness of the purpose of life provides understanding of why we are, where we are in life now and where we need to go next. Without this awareness life would feel like a big puzzle, the missing pieces of which would remain forever shrouded in mystery. A meaningful life dawns with the quest to get in touch with the hidden power and manifest the unique talent in our day to day activities.

The relentless search for the hidden power has been very rewarding for mankind. The quest has encouraged scientific and technological inventions and innovations that have given us a comfortable style of living. The search has also brought renaissance in the spiritual field, giving us a deeper insight into the nature of the ultimate Reality that sustains life and gives meaning to life. It has also provided us with a broader view of religion as a way of living to overcome pains and sufferings and achieve happiness and peace, forsaking conceit, pride, wrath and lust.

Following different paths saints and sages in quest of the hidden power came to the conclusion that behind the diversity of the changing phenomenal world there is one unchanging eternal, unmanifested Reality that sustains life. There is nothing beyond this unmanifest. The multiplicity of the phenomenal world is merely a series of different aspects of the same Reality.

"Beyond the senses are the objects;
Beyond the object is the mind.
Beyond the mind is the intellect;
Beyond the intellect is the unmanifest.
This is the end.
There is nothing beyond."
Katha Upanishad 1:3:10

This unmanifested Reality beyond human intellect and senses has been called by various names: God, Brahman, Truth, Consciousness.

"The Reality is one; sages call it by various names."
The Rigved 1-146-64

The unmanifested Reality pervades everything of this universe. This means it must be present within each one of us. This individualized Divinity within is our real Self, our natural state and the Reality of life. The most startling conclusion of the quest is that God and the Self are one and the same Reality. There is only one Self that pervades all beings. This means that we are not separate. We all are connected to the same Self. We are one. This oneness behind the manifested diversity is the plan of the creation.

"The Self is the Lord of all beings,
The king of all kings
As the spokes are held together
In the hub of a wheel,
Just so all beings,
All creatures, all gods
All worlds and all lives
Are held together in Self."
Brihadaranyaka Upanishad 2:5:15

The two realities—the outer and the inner realities—have complicated our existence. In the outer reality every human being is dominated by the mind and his actions are influenced by ego, lust and selfishness. In the outer reality man-made morality and ethics are the laws that mold his character and conduct and assist him to discriminate between right and wrong. The outer reality creates desire for more wealth, power, fame, and position which are devoid of a point of satiation. The more we get, the more we want. Besides they are not exclusive. You can gain or lose them. Adverse competition to maintain status-quo brings worry, selfishness, and jealousy. The inner reality has created a deeper law of being and living that is free from ego and personal desire. In the inner reality the spiritual power reshapes every aspect of human character and conduct to a divine nature and the whole life undergoes a dramatic uplifting to the delight of the existences. We have to live in this world and cannot transcend the outer reality and live only in the inner reality. The best way to a better living is to harmonize the two realities by performing the duties of life with the principles of the Inner Truth. This means we first firmly entrance ourselves in morality and ethics and then take a trip to the spiritual domain of the inner world to explore who we really are. Without knowing ourselves it is fruitless to try to know others.

The Self cannot make itself known unless your actions are in perfect harmony with your natural state and you make yourself commensurable with it.

> *"The Self, the immortal Spirit,*
> *Resides in the heart of all beings,*
> *Who makes himself free from selfish desires*
> *And the craving of the senses*
> *He beholds the greatness of the Spirit*
> *Through the tranquility of the mind."*
>
> Katha Upanishad 1:2:20

To realize your Self is the most rewarding experience of life. To realize the Self we must accept life as a dynamic integrated state of physical, mental, social, environmental, and spiritual states of existences. This integration is possible by our effort and by the grace of God. Although grace is meshed in the texture of life, grace does not reveal itself unless we toil for it and make ourselves eligible to receive it.

"Ask and it shall be given you
Seek and ye shall find;
Knock and it shall be opened unto you."
                                    St. Matthew 7:7

If you choose a way of living that is not conducive to your growth, it will cut you off from the inner power and lead to depression, boredom, loneliness, and ruin your health in spite of financial affluency and best possible health care.

The Divinity within has also made us spiritual beings of eternal delight. You are not the body, you are not the mind. You are the Self—the Spirit of strength, wisdom, love, and perfection. You are pure, divine, and infinite. There is no limit to what you can do. You can be what you want to be. There is no barrier between you and God. You are one with Him.

"For He is our peace, who hath made
both one, and hath broken down the middle wall of
partition between us."
                                    Ephesians 2:14

Although Divinity within cannot be demonstrated by the conventional methods, it can be intimately experienced. You can get a momentary feeling of this experience when you leave far behind the hustle and bustle of an urban life and unite yourself with the rhythm of the beauty and serenity of nature. Some time watching the roaring waves of a mighty ocean breaking on the beach, or gazing at the twinkling stars in the darkness of the night or looking at the beauty of a snow covered mountain sparks within us a kinship with nature and rouses a profound sense of holiness and the unity of the existences. These feelings of purity and delight are the glimpses of the Divinity within that waits for an opportune moment to come out of the coverings of ignorance and enlighten us with the deepest wisdom of human consciousness.

The degradation of our society today stems mainly from the lack of awareness of what is within us. Being ignorant of our true nature, we seek external solutions to the problems rooted within. In our search for security and prosperity we have abandoned ourselves and are constantly drifting away from human values and virtues. Not by legislation but by a change in the way of living, we can stop this drifting to the degree that we align ourselves with the inner Divinity.

"God abides in the heart of all beings,
But due to our ignorance,
He seems so far, so unreal,
And we move here and there
In search of God
Like a lifeless doll
Mounted on a machine."
                                        The Gita 18:61

We are all spiritual beings
        In human form
Divinity within helps
        To ward off dreary storm.
Letting ourselves be what we truly are
        We realize the spiritual nature of our being
When the Inner Being guides our actions
        Life becomes an expression of Divine blessing.
When you drift away
        From the inner divine center
Quickly return to spiritual course
        To reach the Master.

You are potentially divine. To get back to your divine natural state you have to change following the commandments of the Inner Being. When you change, the Inner Divinity begins to respond in a mysterious way to what you need to return to the essence of being human and experience the oneness of all beings. This expanded vision of life alters the mind, changes character, and brings a sense of belonging in the world. You feel at home. It makes you conscious of your values and priorities and gives a solid foundation to self-confidence and self-esteem. The chaotic problems of life then quickly dissipate.

The life becomes more satisfying and flows with ease, beaming with joy and laughter. This is the indication that the spiritual forces have taken hold of your life and are producing miracles.

Give Life a Spiritual Foundation

Many of us have the false idea that spirituality characterizes a secluded way of life, contemplating on some absolute concepts in the solitude of a remote mountain cave. Hence, it is considered as being the domain of priests, monks and nuns— not of house holders. This cannot be further from truth. Spirituality is for every one. It is the very essence of our being. It is the most practical and natural way of living in harmony with the innermost Truth of our being. It is the only safety against a wrong turn in life. Life becomes meaningful only when it is built on a spiritual foundation. Harmony between the outer and inner realities becomes vibrant and lively when the life is built on a spiritual base. Spirituality is a transformation into our real nature. Spiritual understanding is a direct inspiration from the Divine. It is the practice of the Presence of God.

"Keep thy foot when thou goest
to the house of God,
And be more ready to hear
Than to give the sacrifice of fools
For they consider not that they do evil."
Ecclesiastes 5:1

Spirituality is the most natural way
    To meet the challenges of trial and strife
Contact with the higher power
    Fills the inner void and brings joy to life.
Spirituality is not a fanciful sphere
    Of the transcendental state of being
It is the divine delight
    That comes from love, devotion, and understanding.
Spiritual life is the expression
    Of absolute goodness, truth and beauty
It is the emblem of the
    Living Presence of the Almighty.

9

Spiritual commandments are not man-made
    Laws of ethics and morality
They are messages of growth
    Coming directly from the inner Divinity.
People may have different faiths
    But the spiritual commandments are the same
Because the Reality is one
    Although we call It by various names.

Spirituality does not mean doing anything extraordinary. We are on the spiritual path when we learn to see every day happenings in a new way and make the ordinary events of every day domestic life an opportunity to learn, grow, love, and find delight. Finding delight in doing mere household chores with your whole heart—cooking dinner, washing dishes, watering plants, singing, dancing, spending time with the family—is good spiritual exercise. These activities provide us with the opportunity to feel the infinite within the finite, to see the big within the small, and to understand the profound interconnection and interdependence of all things and beings around us.

Our lives cannot be separated from the world we live in. Unfortunately, in the name of spirituality we have separated the two aspects of life—the inner and the outer needs. This is the root of our problems and pains. True spirituality responds to the wholeness of life by maintaining inner peace and caring for the world we live in—serving those who are hungry and helpless.

Spirituality is not an escape from life
    But an opening for a deeper wisdom
It is in its essence an inner awakening
    To infinite love, joy, and freedom.
Inner spiritual awakening makes us conscious
    Of the two sides of existence
To care for the world around
    And go inside for peace.

A spiritual person is self-controlled
And he maintains calmness in adversity
He is friendly, forgiving
And is devoted to the welfare of humanity.
Following spiritual disciplines
One becomes free from fear and anger
And acquires a peaceful equanimity
Overcoming passion and selfish desire.
Integrate spiritual disciplines
With the affairs of everyday living
You will realize God
And the joy of divine blessing.

Honesty

Spiritual journey to perfection begins with your honesty. You have to be honest with yourself and with the people. When we are dishonest with ourselves and with others, we create an inner turbulence that destroys the link with the Inner Divinity and we pay a terrible price for the deceitful act. To be honest you have to align your actions with your heart. Complete honesty and consistency in speech, mind, and action is the key to spiritual growth and the true enduring characteristic of a successful person.

Honesty is telling the truth
    And admitting when you are wrong
Free from fear and anger
    Honest living is a pleasant song.
What you do to others
    Soon comes back to you
This is the law of nature
    And always holds true.
Honesty is treating everyone with fairness
    And with a blissful equanimity
Honesty may not bring wealth
    But makes you the joy of humanity.
Be consistent in all
    Your speech, thought, and action
You will gain friendship
    And success in your mission.

Responsibility

A journey to perfection cannot be undertaken unless you take responsibility for your own life. We know ourselves better and become responsible citizens when we take charge of our own lives. Taking responsibility for our own lives will erase the sense of dependence and give you self confidence. It will empower you to be creative to face the challenges of life. Responsible persons are those who know that the circumstances they arc in are products of their own conscious choices. To blame others for your misfortune is a sign of immaturity. Blaming others is a negative attitude and hampers progress. You are responsible for your happiness or unhappiness. The quality of a person's life is directly proportional to the degree of responsibility he takes for his own life and the commitment he makes to change for the better. This total dedication is the key to perfection and that is what life is all about.

> Responsibility is the sign
> Of maturity to function
> To take charge of life
> And resist temptation.
> Blaming others for your misfortune
> Is a great misunderstanding
> Perceive your true value
> And begin a new beginning.

Pains and Sufferings

The road to spiritual journey is bumpy and many times you may face overwhelming pains and sufferings. Pains and sufferings are, of course, not obstacles but divine gifts to grow physically, mentally and spiritually. You will not go anywhere if you run away from them. Face them and accept the challenges of life. Tragedies contain seeds of great potent forces that can open you to a new awakening and transform life for the better. Pains and sufferings force us to straighten the priorities of life and return to love when we drift away from it.

The origin and the true purpose of pains and sufferings are shrouded in mystery. The quest to find an answer to the question, "Why this tragedy?" or "Why not?" is bound to end up in frustration. Don't try to find an answer to these questions from the level of normal human consciousness. You will not find an answer. When you rise above the reasoning faculty of human intellect these questions vanish. No one, not even a saint, can avoid pains and sufferings. The saints, by their spiritual way of living, develop enormous courage, strength, and wisdom and reach an altogether new level of fortitude, patience and equanimity. They accept suffering but respond to it in such a way as to transform the perception of pain to an opportunity to learn and to grow.

Chaos breeds the seed of the new order. This is the law of nature. Wisdom is the reward in disguise of all human tragedies. Crises and tragedies bring us closer to each other and focus light to see the inside of us. We transcend our differences and feel the interconnection of things and beings. Living in the law of the outer life we cannot avoid pains and sufferings. The only way to over come pains and sufferings is to turn inward. Through the experience of the Inner Truth one's whole life undergoes an inconceivable change for the better. We transcend pain and wake up to love, joy of oneness of all things and beings of His creation.

14

"When the whole variety of beings
He perceives as resting on the One
And is an evolution from that One
Then he transcends pains and sufferings
And gets united with the essence
Of delight and existence."

The Gita 13:30

"Mortal verily is the body gripped by death, but within it dwells the immortal Self. The Self when associated in our consciousness with the body, is subject to pleasure and pain; and so long as this association continues there is no cessation of pleasure and pain. But neither pleasure nor pain touches one who is not identified with the Body."

"Rising above physical consciousness—knowing the Self as distinct from the sense and the mind—one becomes free of pain."

Chandogya Upanishad 8:12:1 and 3

Patience Is the Key to Self Improvement

Patience is a unique spiritual device
　　To cope with strife and feel His Presence.
Rooted in love and compassionate thought
　　It kills hatred and imparts lessons of endurance.

Patience is a mighty power, an admirable virtue and a great asset in life. Patience is an acquired virtue and can be achieved by controlling the mind and the sense organs.

Did you grumble when you were standing in a long line on a hot summer day?

Did you complain when the waiter in the restaurant was slow in serving you?

Did you express your frustration and anger when you failed to fix the kitchen faucet?

If your answer is "no," you are on your way to acquiring a great skill, a great strength, a great virtue called Patience.

Nature is our teacher on earth
　　To give lessons of patience and endurance,
Trees bear the winter and wait
　　For the spring to change their appearance.
Change is the plan of the creation
　　And nothing would last forever,
To get what we need
　　We have to learn to wait and bear.
Everything in nature
　　changes in a cyclic order,
Each one has a season
　　And never steps on each other.

"To everything
There is a season,
And a time to every purpose
Under the heaven."
Ecclesiastes 3:1

16

Be patient and still and learn the act of endurance. Your pain cannot last forever. Through your patience and endurance you will acquire the skill to harmonize life with the rhythm of the changing universe. You will then see and hear sounds that will open your mind and expand your vision.

"Open thou mine eyes, that I may behold
Wondrous things out of Thy law."
Psalm 119:18

"Feelings of heat and cold
Pleasure and pain
Are caused by the contact
Of the sense organs
With the sense-objects
They come and they go,
Never lasts forever.
You must be patient
And learn to put up with them."
The Gita 2:14

Patience is needed to understand the key issues of your children. If you want to make a point to your children, you have to be patient and first listen to what your children are saying. Don't get impatient with them and don't rush them. Otherwise you will damage the relationship and spoil everything. You will be understood better if you first listen to them and understand them. You will be able to communicate with them much more freely and peacefully if you are patient.

Patience is rooted in love and compassion. It is the outcome of unconditional love. If you love and care for some one, you will be automatically patient with that person. Due to our impatience, we often do not take time to understand a person— we are quick to criticize. Have patience, strive to understand the person and the situation he is in before you jump to a conclusion.

"Judge not, and ye shall not be judged,
condemn not, and ye shall not be condemned.
Forgive, and ye shall be forgiven."
St. Luke 6:37

"Judge not according to appearance,
but judge righteous judgement."
John 7:24

Don't run a race to become spiritually perfect overnight. Don't be a victim of the instant fad. Quick fix is an illusion. You cannot be perfect in an instant. Be patient with yourself. Take your time to do the best you can. Do not get depressed if you make a mistake or fail in your first attempt. Accept failure or a mistake as an opportunity to learn and to be better in the future. Develop a positive attitude and don't rush for time or the result.

Increase patience by your will
And lots of practice
To have joy at home
And peace in the office.

Don't expect a miracle to happen. Self-improvement is a life long undertaking. Don't put a time table on your journey to perfection. Be patient and try to change a little at a time.

Great achievements
Were not accomplished in a day
Patience and perseverance
Prevailed throughout the way.
Doing a little at a time
Is the great art of living
It is the way to perfection
That leads to inner being.

Internal transformation is a very slow process and the journey is challenging. No one can tread this path for you. You have to take the trip all by yourself. Don't count on others to live your life for you.

> *"No one can help you grow but yourself*
> *No one can let you down but yourself*
> *You are your friend you are your enemy."*
> The Gita 6:5

Don't be scared to accept the challenges of life. Many people do not feel the delight of existence because they are scared to accept the challenges and uncertainties of life. They conform to the outdated customs simply because they feel familiar and it gives them a sense of security. They do not have the strength to tolerate insecurities and the courage to challenge the status quo. They mold themselves to the expectations and opinions of others and suffer from the stress and frustrations of an unfulfilled life.

> *"Do not be conformed to this world,*
> *but be transformed*
> *to the renewal of your mind*
> *that you may prove*
> *what is the will of God*
> *what is good and acceptable and perfect."*
> Romans 12:2

Don't worry; every piece of the puzzle will fall into place if you change in a constructive and positive way. Ask for divine guidance for wisdom and patience to maintain tranquility and peace in conflicts and chaos.

> *"Oh Lord, grant us the serenity*
> *To accept things we cannot change*
> *The courage to change the things we can*
> *And the wisdom to know the difference."*
> *Amen*

Faith

Another ingredient necessary for self-improvement is faith in yourself—faith is your Inner Divinity.

> Faith is a marvelous moving force
> That empowers you night and day
> It shows the path to meet the challenges
> That come your way.

Faith is the driving force of life capable of bringing new experiences that otherwise would seem impossible. Upanishad says that the subtle essence that sustains life and propels the universe is the invisible Self and "Thou Art That." You are the universe. Realize this profound statement and have faith in yourself. Your inner power will then work for you.

This faith is not just hoping or believing. It is the truth of your being and becoming. It is a direct recognition and surrender to the power greater than yours. It is an invitation to the Divinity within to take over and control your life so that you can grow in it and become it.

> *"In accord with the natural disposition*
> *Of every person*
> *Is his faith.*
> *A person is verily made up of faith*
> *As a person's faith is*
> *So is he or she."*
> The Gita 17:3

> *"Those without faith in My knowledge*
> *Shall fail to find Me*
> *Back they must return On the path of endless*
> *Rounds of births and deaths."*
> The Gita 9:3

Through your faith and will you can overcome your weaknesses and shortcomings to the point where you can be what you want to be. The difference between success and failure is not the lack of knowledge but lack of faith and determination. The universe has no separate existence apart from the human being. The person, who realizes that the universe proceeds from the secret place of his heart gets rid of ignorance and attains supreme equality with the Lord.

"The man of faith
Whose heart is devoted
Whose senses are mastered
Overcomes trials and tribulations of life
And passes to the highest state
Of supreme peace.
The ignorant, the doubter, the faithless perish
There is no happiness for him
Either in this world or the next."
The Gita 4:39 and 40

Through your faith you will know what you have to do to meet the challenges of life and develop a personal relationship with the Divine to make a leap from the state of self-imposed limitations to a more expanded vision of life's infinite possibilities. Keep your faith alive and put it in practice. It will remove fear, give you security and faith in others.

Faith in yourself is the Spirit of life
    And the secret of greatness
It helps to get what you need
    Removes fear and always brings success.
When darkness covers the rocky path
    And it seems you are not going anywhere
Don't give up, have faith in yourself
    Hope will blossom and light will be there.
When you say that you cannot do the job
    Due to lack of proper ability
It only means that you don't know yourself
    And are ignorant of your infinite potentiality.

21

Faith in your Inner Divinity is nothing but practicing the Presence of God. You will be in perfect peace, health, and happiness when you are in His Presence. Because these are His blessings. Forget your problems and seek first the grace of the Lord. God will work for you because you have taken refuge in Him.

> *"Take no thought for your life,*
> *What ye shall eat,*
> *Or what ye shall drink,*
> *Nor yet for your body*
> *What ye shall put on.*
> *Your heavenly Father knoweth*
> *That ye have need*
> *For all those things.*
> *Seek ye first the kingdom of God*
> *And his righteousness*
> *And all these things*
> *Shall be added unto you."*
> St. Matthew 6:31-34

Faith needs to be nurtured to counteract the divisive forces that destroy the harmony of the outer and the inner realities of life and make us forgetful of what we truly are. We have to affirm again and again our divine nature until we can make the Inner Power to work for us.

Go in some solitary place and remain quiet for a couple of minutes. Then repeat the following affirmations till they become part of your New You. With this spiritual awakening you will know yourself better and experience the hidden forces filling your mind with courage, hope, joy and freedom.

> I am not the body, nor the mind
> I am the unchanging eternal Self
> While crossing the rough and rugged path
> I get a lot of It's help.
> I am pure, perfect, and divine.

I am strength, knowledge and bliss
Controlling my desire and senses
I am free from fear and anxieties
Work always gives me satisfaction
As I dedicate its fruit to God
I overcome sorrows and pains
With the grace of my beloved Lord.
I have complete trust
In the Truth of my Inner Being
It gives me peace of mind
and the joy of living.

Pointers for a New Beginning

The reality of life—our Self
  Resides in the heart of all beings.
Perform your duties with the inner principles
  And experience the essence of all things.
Take responsibility for your life
  And make a commitment to change for the better
You will rise above fear and anger
  With faith and lots of prayer.
Give life a spiritual foundation
  With honesty and consistency in speech and action
And learn the art of endurance
  To avoid frustration and to achieve perfection.
Self-improvement is a life long process
  Never put a time table for this endeavor
Be patient, keep your faith alive
  And worship God with things you most favor.
Follow these pointers to the best of your ability
  And ask for God's blessing
You will be ready for a fresh start
  And to begin a new beginning.

> *"Lead me in thy truth,*
> *And teach me:*
> *For thou art the God of my salvation*
> *On thee do I wait all day."*
> Psalms 25:5

Persistently practice the following principles to achieve a satisfying and meaningful life.

1. Take responsibility for your own life. The quality of a person's life is directly proportional to the degree of responsibility he takes for his own life and makes a commitment to change for the better. Don't be afraid of pains and sufferings. They are divine gifts for our growth. Accept suffering, but respond to it in such a way as to transform the perception of

pain to an opportunity to learn.

2. Have faith in your inner power. Faith in your inner power opens the door to new experiences and makes good things come to you which otherwise would seem impossible. Through your faith you can overcome your weaknesses and shortcomings to the point where you can meet the challenges of life. Affirm consciously to be connected with your inner source of infinite love, wisdom, and joy. Your affirmation will be made manifest in your life and you will be what you want to be.

3. Give life a spiritual foundation to respond to the wholeness of life by satisfying your inner and outer needs. It will energize your life and give you the vitality to free yourself of the negative attitude and fulfill your hopes and ambitions.

4. Be honest with yourself and with others. Complete honesty in speech, mind, and action is the key to your growth and the true enduring characteristic of a successful person.

5. Be patient and learn the art of endurance. Control your mind and live a relaxed life in the midst of trials and tribulations.

6. Life is growth and growth means change. Change yourself to lead a meaningful life.

"I will instruct thee and teach thee
In the way which thou should go:
I will guide thee with mine eye."
Psalm 32:8

II
Alter the Pattern of Your Thinking

"Except ye be converted
And become his little children,
Ye shall not enter into
The kingdom of heaven."
                    St. Matthew 18:3

Thoughts are born
  In the depths of the mind
And give rise to
  Relentless desires of all kind.
The endless desire for more
  Cannot give you satisfaction
They kill the virtues
  And block the way to perfection.
Getting more makes us happier
  Is a belief of delusion
Insatiable desire for more
  Cannot be quenched by earthly possession.
Satisfy one desire
  And a new one takes its place
The endless parade of desires
  Are very hard to efface.
Alter the pattern of your thoughts
  To avoid a lot of sorrow
Give up the idea of ownership
  And allow your mind to grow.
Anger and selfish desire
  Are the sources of worldly pain and misery
Master these impulses
  And realize existence as a reflection of His glory.
Do not pollute the heart
  With selfish desire
To achieve peace and joy
  That last forever.

Desire

"A person consists of desires
As his desire so is his will;
As his will, so is the deed he does,
Whatever deed he does,
That is his destiny.
The doer of good becomes good,
The doer of evil becomes evil
One becomes virtuous by virtuous action
Bad by bad action.
When all desires
That dwell in the heart
Are cast away,
Then does the mortal become immortal.
Who is freed from desire
Whose desire is satisfied
Whose desire is to attain the Self
He merges with the Supreme Lord."
                    Brihadaranyaka Upanishad 4:4-7

"The cause of all suffering
Is rooted in desire
If the desire is extinguished
Suffering has no foot hold."
                    The Mahayana Religious Ideal

Human beings are blessed to have a unique faculty called the mind. It is the place where the thoughts are born. You are the reflection of your thoughts. The thoughts in your mind have the tendency to actualize. You see what you think. You dream what you think and you become what you think. By controlling the mind, the destructive thoughts can be filtered out and replaced by thoughts that are loving, kind, and refreshing.

"Be sure to think of noble thoughts
Whatsoever things are honest,
Whatsoever things are just,
Whatsoever things are pure
Whatsoever things are lovely
Whatsoever things are of good report
If there be any virtue,
And if there be any praise,
Think on those things."
Philippians 4:8

"The senses, mind, and intellect
Are the abode of selfish desire
That obscures knowledge and understanding
Therefore you must control
Your sense, mind, and intellect
And then conquer the evils
That stand in your way
To know yourself."
The Gita 3:40 and 41

"Love not the world,
Neither the things that are in the world
If any man love the world
The love of the Father is not in him.
For all that is in the world,
The lust of flesh
And the lust of the eyes
And the pride of life
Is not the Father
But is of the world."
John 2:15 and 16

Constant thoughts of worldly possessions, if not curtailed, may cause your downfall. Remember, you cannot get everything you want. Control your desire and you will see that you don't need those things you wanted so much.

"When you keep thinking
About sense objects
Attachment comes.
Attachment breeds addiction,
Thwart your addiction
It turns to anger.
Anger clouds your judgement
And confuses your mind.
Confuse your mind,
You forget lessons of past experiences
Forget experiences,
You lose discrimination
And your life is utter waste."
The Gita 2:62 and 63

Selfish desires always encourage immoral practices. To ward off desire for personal gratification, regard others as yourself and be compassionate and useful to all beings.

"Not hater of any living creature
Friendly and compassionate to all
Free from selfish desire
And the delusion of "I" and "Mine"
Indifferent to pain and pleasure
Patient and forgiving,
This disciplined person
Who is ever content
Whose self is controlled of firm resolve
Whose thoughts and intellect
Are dedicated to Me,
Is dear to Me."
The Gita 12:13 and 14

31

Anger

Desire is insatiable. The more we get, the more we want. The more you run after desires, the more you get frustrated. Unfulfilled desire is the cause of anger. Anger is a great obstacle to growth. Do not be a victim to the impulse of anger. Don't act in the heat of the moment. Take it easy and be patient. You may not be right all the time. Don't cling to things that are not yours. Have a detached attitude and a feeling of love, compassion, and forgiveness toward all.

> *"Desire, wrath, and greed*
> *Are the three fold gate to hell*
> *Leading to the ruin of the soul.*
> *Hence one should abandon these three.*
> *Freed from these three gates of darkness*
> *A person achieves joy and freedom*
> *Reaching the highest level of perfection."*
>
> The Gita 16:21 and 22

> *"Abandoning all desires*
> *And free from ego, pride, and anger*
> *A person attains peace."*
>
> The Gita 2:71

Don't allow anger to grow. When you allow anger to prolong or to intensify, it produces hatred. Put your trust in God and have a strong determination not to be carried away by your emotion. In case of an altercation, the Bible recommends reconciliation even before worshipping God.

> *"Whosoever is angry with his brother without cause*
> *Shall be in the danger of the judgement.*
> *Therefore if thou bring thy gift to the alter,*
> *And there rememberest*
> *That thy brother hath ought against thee.*
> *Leave there thy gift before the alter*

And go thy way;
First be reconciled to thy brother
And then come and offer thy gift."
St. Matthew 5:22-24

"If a man say, I love God,
And hateth his brother,
He is a liar;
For he that loveth not his brother
Whom he hath seen,
How can he love God
Whom he hath not seen?"
1 John 4:20

"Controlling the mind and intelligence
And freed from selfish desire, fear, and anger
Who seeks freedom
Truly that person is free forever."
The Gita 5:28

"Freed from both lust and anger
A person can move safely
Amidst the world of senses
All sorrows then melt
In the peaceful joy of living
With the Indwelling Spirit."
The Gita 2:64 and 65

The natural cure for anger
　　Comes by cultivating the spirit of humility
Because humility in its essence
　　Is love of God and perfect sublimity.
Humility does not cast you down
　　But raises the soul above imperfection
Humility is rooted in inner strength
　　And cleanses the heart of passion.
Humility makes us conscious

Of the qualities we are lacking
And prevents us from boasting
For the talent we are having.
How insignificantly little we feel
Beholding the vastness of the creation
This experience of nothingness
Brings humility in our attitude and action.

"Let not the wise man boast of his wisdom
Or the strong man boast of his strength
Or the rich man boast of his riches,
but let him who boast about this
That he understands and knows Me
That I am the lord.
Who exercises kindness, justice
And righteousness on earth,
For in these I delight."
Jeremiah 9:23 and 24

Developing a Detached Attitude

Detachment is a way of looking at things
  To overcome the desire of possession
It gives you freedom and faith
  To move peacefully amidst the world of passion.
Detachment is not abandoning the family and friend
  And living in solitude as a hermit
It is an inner transformation and enlightenment
  To be in this world but not of it.
Detachment means giving up the idea
  That you deserve more than others
It provides a new way
  To cope with stress and insatiable desires.
Detachment also means sharing your good fortune
  With the people who are in poverty
And let them feel that the essence of living
  Is love, joy, and liberty.
Detached attitude is a virtue
  That is not so easy to acquire
Death is the best teacher
  To give the proper lesson you require.
You can take nothing with you
  When death sends the invitation
You then see the real owner
  Of all your earthly possession.
Give without expectation of return
  And help people to regain their dignity
Detached attitude will then be yours
  From these noble acts of charity.

Detachment purifies the heart and burns up the evil effects of our deed. It enlightens us to the point where we become equal minded to all creatures. Detachment, unselfishness, love, and morality go hand in hand. They empower us to gain freedom to overcome pains and sufferings and experience the delight of existence.

"When the heart is made pure
By the practice of detachment
And the senses are mastered
And one sees his or her own Self
As the Self of all creatures,
He or she remains untainted by action."

The Gita 5:7

"Who puts desire aside
And dedicates every action to God
Abandoning attachment
Then he or she is not affected by any action
Just as the lotus leaf
Remains unwetted on water."

The Gita 5:10

"The followers of unattached action
Are self-purified and consider
The body, mind, sense-organs, and the intellect
As instruments only
In the hands of God."

The Gita 5:11

Your will, discrimination, and compassion are your friends
to develop a detached attitude. Pains and sufferings also help
to put you on the right track. When you suffer running after
personal desires and get frustrated, detachment dawns in your
life. Detached attitude also develops from the appreciation of
the philanthropic activities of the great soul. When you realize
the sacrifice of these people for the benefit of others and see
the sufferings and poverty of the people around the world,
suddenly the things you hold so dear don't seem to mean much
any longer, and you progress on the path of detachment.

Actually the idea of ownership is the cause of all our troubles
and misery. There is nothing that belongs to us except our own
Self. Everything belongs to Him. We are His caretakers. "Your
body is not your own," says the Taoist thinker, "it is the

delegated image of God. Your life is not your own, it is the delegated harmony of God. Your individuality is not your own, it is the delegated adaptability of God.

By the detached attitude toward worldly acquisitions a sense of gratitude for what we have overpowers the desire to get what we do not have. We are no longer obsessed with the "I" thoughts and realize that "Thou" and not "I" is the heart of the art of better living. This spiritual awakening relieves us from the sense of self-gratification, possession, hoarding, and selfishness to the profound experience of equal mindedness to all and of being useful to others.

"The Supreme Reality stands revealed
In the consciousness of those
Who have conquered themselves.
They are detached
And are at peace
In cold and heat
In pleasure and pain
In honor and dishonor.
They are completely fulfilled
With wisdom and knowledge.
Having conquered attachments
They climb to the summit
Of human consciousness.
They are equal minded
To relatives, enemy and friend
To some one who supports
And also to one who is hateful."
The Gita 6:7 to 9

Freedom is the goal of life. Without relinquishing attachment you cannot attain freedom. Freedom is the fruit of unselfish acts. Pour out your love and understanding and open your heart and mind to others around you. Don't be over obsessed with your own things. Put the needs, hopes, and aspirations of others above your own. Give freely for its own sake. Expect nothing in return. Enjoy life bringing joy to others. Then will come perfect detached attitude.

> *"When a person achieves non-attachment*
> *Self-control and freedom from desire,*
> *He or she passes beyond*
> *The effects of all actions*
> *And reaches the supreme state*
> *Of perfection and freedom."*
>
> The Gita 18:49

Controlling the Mind

How do you tame the restless wandering mind?

> *"The mind is restless*
> *And difficult to control*
> *But it can be brought under control*
> *Through regular practice*
> *And by the constant exercise of detachment*
> *Those who lack self-control*
> *Will find it difficult*
> *To control the mind*
> *But a self-controlled person*
> *Who strives hard*
> *Can attain the goal."*
>
> The Gita 6:35 and 36

To gain self-control you have to make the mind pure. Purifying the mind does not mean that we create a new mind or we become a saint overnight. It means we must learn to bring our lives out of the land of fantasy. We learn not to identify ourselves with the physical body and impose our liking and disliking on the world. We learn to be what we are right now. Letting ourselves be what we are right now, we touch the divinity within, see our oneness with the whole universe and learn to respond to the challenges of life without being biased by our ego or selfish desire.

> *"Those who rise above*
> *Selfish desire and anger*
> *Through constant effort*
> *And firm determination*
> *Conquer themselves*
> *And gain control*
> *Over passion and mind*
> *They experience the Self*
> *And live forever in Nirvana."*
>
> The Gita 5:26

To calm down, sit comfortably and quietly on a chair. Don't do anything. Just keep a watch on the mind. If the mind does not get any support from you, it will get tired. You can then bring it back to any position you want. The mind will be released from the imprisonment of ignorance and imperfection. It will no longer wander in the world of passion, but will reveal to you everything you need to know to lead a meaningful life.

"Renouncing wholeheartedly
All selfish desire and expectations
Use your firm determination
To control the senses
And the mind.
Keep your mind in rest
And free from
All mental distractions
With the aid of intelligent will.
Little by little
Through patience
And repeated effort
The mind will become fixed
On the Divinity within.
No matter where
The restless mind wonders
It must be drawn back
And led to within to rest
In the Self only.
Abiding joy comes to those
Who still the mind
Conquer the senses
And get free from ego
And unite with the Lord."
The Gita 6:24-27

Taming the mind enables you to keep track of one thing at a time and focus all your attention on the present moment. Your life is the sum total of the present moments. If you miss the present, you miss your life.

40

Observing Periodic Silence

"Be still and know that I am God."
Psalms 46:10

Silence is generally used in the sense of stillness, calmness, quietness, or absence of any sound. The importance of silence in human life cannot be overemphasized. It is like an oasis in a vast arid desert. Unfortunately in the era of noise coming from industry, automobile, plane, radio, and television the word silence seems to be slipping away from the pages of our life.

True silence means both inner and outer quietness. Inner silence renews your spirit and refreshes your mind. You must combine your activity with silence. Spending a little time each day to maintain silence is necessary for increasing your awareness of everything that happens around you.

> Inward silence and detached attitude
>   Are needed to control the mind
> A quiet mind empowers us
>   To resist vices of all kind.
> Silence is the natural way
>   To meet God face to face
> In the sacredness of inward silence
>   You experience the Divine Grace.
> Stillness, calmness, and silence
>   Are not only attempts to express the Infinity
> But they pinpoint also the condition
>   To experience the ultimate Reality.
> In silence you renew
>   Your spiritual strength of life
> That helps you to cope
>   With despair and strife.

Every morning and evening set aside some time and observe complete silence during that period. Just observe the thoughts as they arise in your mind and allow them to pass away quietly

41

without getting involved with them. Keep your awareness sharp by letting go of one thought after another without reacting or judging. You will experience a greater inner calm and a profound refreshing effect by this simple technique throughout your busy schedule. Your consciousness will leap to a higher level. You will rise above prejudices and find solutions to chaotic problems of life. Wherever you go, whatever you do, carry the inner stillness with you all the time to enjoy every moment of your life.

> *"Through the silence of the mind*
> *And the spiritual discipline*
> *You must know Him*
> *Who is higher than consciousness*
> *And destroy your elusive enemy*
> *That has the form of lust."*
>
> The Gita 3:43

Happiness

"The uncontrolled mind
Cannot concentrate
Who cannot concentrate
Has no peace,
Without peace, where is happiness?"
                              The Gita 2:66

Happiness is the very core of our being. We do not get happiness because we are usually looking for happiness in the wrong places. Happiness is the fruit of inner fulfillment. We seek inner fulfillment in sources that are outside of us and pursue happiness that is always somewhere else beyond our reach. Happiness is inside and not outside. Unfortunately our society has taught us to conform to the idea that fulfillment depends on outer achievements. This is why we seek happiness in wealth, fame, power, sex, and drugs. To be happy you have to change your pattern of thinking. Happiness comes not from giving up desires but by controlling desires and passions.

Happiness comes from the fulfillment of our physical, mental, and spiritual needs. It comes from the virtues and of being useful to others. It comes from forgiveness, charity, and all the noble acts that activate peace of mind and trigger joy.

Happiness is not a commercial commodity
    Available for buying or selling.
It is a state of mind
    That comes from spiritual awakening.
Spiritual awakening brings along
    A profound gift of inward calmness
From this peace of mind
    Is born ever lasting happiness.
If you pursue happiness
    As the ultimate goal of your living
You will be drifting away
    From happiness and your real being.

Happiness is not a transcendental state of mind
    That is very difficult to have
It is the joyful expression of enlightened mind
    And is born of unconditional love.
Don't seek happiness
    Trying to change the world you live in
Change yourself first
    Otherwise your efforts will bring lots of pain.
To be happy you need not be
    A distinguished scholar or a millionaire
Happiness is your very being
    And does not depend on wealth or attire.
To be happy here you need not be
    A world leader or a business tycoon
Bring the inner virtues out into the world
    And you get happiness as a boon.
He is happy who puts the past behind
    And is grateful for the things he is enjoying
He is not scared of the problems of life
    Difficulties he considers as opportunities for growing.
He rejoices in the well-being of others
    And loves to serve everyone with pleasure
He is aware of the oneness of beings
    and is conscious of what we truly are.
He is not a slave
    Of addiction, obsession, or emotions
And is aware of his
    Worldly duties and spiritual obligations.
He is self-controlled and is free
    From the craving of getting this or that
He has no fear or anger
    And is equal minded to people, dog or cat.

Pointers for Noble Thoughts

You are what you are thinking
   Day and night
Worldly thoughts breed selfish desire
   And obscure divine light.
It is not the event but the perception of it
   That can inspire or frighten you
Because you see the world the way you think
   And get a right or a wrong view.
When the road is bumpy
   You think that life is all suffering.
Change the way you are thinking
   And experience the joy of living.
Wealth, power, name, and fame
   Can be gained or lost at any time
Give up attachment to deceptive things
   And think of thoughts that are divine.
Control the restless mind by constant practice
   And rise over ego and passion
Develop a detached attitude and observe periodic silence
   To achieve freedom and salvation.
Detachment is rooted in the Divinity within
   Go inside and master this divine quality
And develop the spirit of giving
   To get the taste of joy and liberty.

Persistently practice the following principles to achieve a satisfying and meaningful life.

1. You are the reflection of your thoughts. Mind is the place where thoughts are born. Control the mind to filter out destructive thoughts and replace them with thoughts that are loving, kind and refreshing.

2. Desire—an emotion that satisfies itself through the senses and manifests through the wish for possession and enjoyment—is insatiable. Frustration and anger are the results of unfulfilled desire. Don't be a victim of the impulse of anger. Don't allow

anger to grow or prolong. Put your trust in God and change your feeling and perception of the event. Have a strong determination not to be carried away by your emotion.

3. Don't be over obsessed with your own things. Put the needs, hopes, and aspirations of others above your own. Give freely without expecting a return. Then will come the perfect detached attitude that will purify your heart and empower you to overcome pains and sufferings.

4. By constant practice and detached attitude learn to control the mind and bring it from the land of fantasy to where you are right now and focus all your attention on the present moment. Letting yourself be one with what you are doing now will block the distracting thoughts that make you restless.

5. Learn not to identify yourself with the physical body and impose your liking and disliking on the world. Learn to respond to the challenges of life without being biased by ego or selfish desire. Your perception of unselfish services and wholeness of life will change also the negative attitude of the people around you.

6. Spend a little time each day to observe silence wherever you go, whatever you do, carry the inner silence with you all the time. You will see miracles happening in your life.

"Let noble thoughts
Come to us
From every side."
Rig Veda 1:89:1

III
Love and Serve All Beings

"If we love one another
God dwelleth in us
And his love is perfected in us."
1 John 4:12

Love and Serve All Beings

Love is the creative power of the universe
   That manifests as strength and beauty
To love is to know God
   And the inmost nature of the ultimate Reality.
Love is the life of the virtues
   And a profound feeling of association
Love finds harmony in the inconsistencies of life
   And faces difficulties with compassion.
To love and to be loved
   Are every one's hope and sincere aspiration
All the commandments are in love
   It is therefore the way to salvation.
Love is a great transformative force
   That brings hope in despair and joy in sorrow
So love and take care of all beings now
   And never wait for tomorrow.
Each and every human being is a visible form
   Of the invisible, eternal, divine Reality
Travel the wide open road of love
   And discover the oneness of God and humanity.
All life is one and the same Spirit
   Pervades the immense creation of God
Love and regard every being
   They are the image of the same good Lord.
Love is the miraculous power of God
   That paves the road to forgiveness
It shows how to give freely
   And rise to higher levels of consciousness.
Not by fire arms, nor by legislation
   But by the power of love
Peace will come amongst nations
   And the harmony every one likes to have.
With boundless love and compassion
   Perform every act of charity
You will get a glimpse now
   Of the enigmatic Reality.

"He that loveth not
Knoweth not God
For God is love."
1 John 4:8

God is the Reality of life and love is the emblem of this divine Reality. Creation is a manifestation of this love. Human love is the glimpse of the purity and perfection of divine love. Without the love of God human love has no separate existence. Fulfillment of life is the fruit of obeying the commandments coming from the sweetness and strength of love.

"Behold, let us love one another;
for love is God;
And every one that loveth is born of God,
and knoweth God."
1 John 4:7

Love consecrates life and provides opportunities for spiritual awakening from the state of separation to the state of oneness where there is no duality. By letting go of separateness we see love as the connecting link with all beings and perceive others as the reflection of our own self and harmony in the inconsistencies and imperfections of the existence and explore joy in the midst of the pains and problems of life.

"Who sees all beings in himself
And himself in all beings
And constantly meditates on God,
Such a disciplined person
Reaches the Lord and enjoys boundless bliss."
The Gita 6:28 and 29

Love and Equality

It is through the miraculous power of love that we acquire the profound virtue of equanimity—the ability to accept equally the vibrations of the dualities of nature—pain and pleasure, defeat and victory, failure and success, grief and joy, and grow into our real being. Gita gives a vivid portrait of a person poised in equality.

"He sees with an equal eye,
The learned and the illiterate
The cow, the elephant, the dog
And the outcast."

The Gita 5:18

"His mind is untroubled by sorrows
And by the desires of pleasures
He has no likes or dislikes
And is above passion, fear, and rage.
He remains calm in all situations,
Neither rejoices nor detests
And accepts without excitement
Whatever comes good or evil, pain or pleasure
He withdraws his senses
From the sense objects
As a tortoise withdraws
His limbs into the shell."

The Gita 2:57 and 58

Starting from the small events of day to day life, equality can be developed through the power of endurance and will. In due course it will make you indifferent to the contacts and impacts of the dualities of life and provide sufficient momentum to tide over the most adverse circumstances. Instead of reacting violently to an adverse situation you will have the ability to get hold of the situation with patience and understanding. You will not be a victim of your ego and selfish desire.

50

"Those who are free
From any sense of duality
Are unaffected by likes and dislikes
And are free
From the bondage of ego and selfish desire."
The Gita 5:3

The secret of establishing mental equanimity is to extend your love and get control of your mind and the senses.

"Our senses have been conditioned
By attraction to the pleasant
And an aversion to the unpleasant.
Do not be ruled by them
They are obstacles to your growth."
The Gita 3:34

The final step in this endeavor is the submission of the individual will to the will of God for a union of the soul with the Divine. This union—the result of unconditional love and devotion—is the meaning of freedom and the secret of perfect equanimity.

"Thou shalt love the Lord thy God
With all thy heart
And with all thy soul
And with all thy strength
And with all thy mind;
And thy neighbor as thyself."
St. Luke 10:27

Love is not something extraneous that we need to create. It is the essence of our being. No one can take away this precious gift from us. It is what we are born with. From love we come, by love we exit, and to love we return. Love defies the law of arithmetic. It never decreases but always increases through giving. The more you give the more it becomes. Love never grows old. It is timeless and perpetually unveils the wonders of life.

> Love—the band of perfection
> Is the glimpse of the Lord
> Feel the fullness and abundance
> Of this precious gift from God.
> Who loves all beings
> And treats them as his deity
> He has the greatest idea
> Of worshiping the invisible Infinity.
> By love we get the divine grace
> To go beyond human potentiality
> And reach the highest goal of life
> Union with the ultimate Reality.

Love is the life of all the virtues. Without love there can be no beauty or goodness in any of the virtues. Apart from love it is impossible to understand the spirit of self sacrifice—those who suffer and sacrifice their lives even embrace death for the good of others. When Jesus Christ was being nailed and facing death, he prayed, *"Father forgive them for they know not what they do."* This spirit of incredible sacrifice is an expression of the love that transcends human consciousness. Love does not judge, does not criticize and asks no questions. Because of these qualities love has a miraculous healing power.

If you always judge and criticize people, you will have no time to love them. Do not become a fault-finder. Become a love-finder. See the goodness and strength of others and overlook their imperfections and weaknesses. Judgement blinds us. Love restores the sight immediately and takes us beyond fear and worry.

Love Is Letting Go of Fear and Worry

"For God hath not given us the spirit of fear;
But of power, and of love and of a sound mind."
II Timothy 1:7

Fear and worry are not real. They are creations of an ignorant mind. A disciplined mind can counteract the gloomy feelings of fear and worry by entertaining noble thoughts of love and compassion.

"There is no fear in love;
But perfect love casteth out fear;
Because fear hath torment.
He that feareth
Is not made perfect in love."
1 John 4:18

Negative thoughts create conditions conducive to the actualization of that which you fear and the things you fear are likely to come to you sooner or later. Instead of dwelling on the negative forces, focus your attention on the positive ideas that will give you strength and courage. The best antidote to fear and worry is the awareness of the infinite strength, wisdom, and bliss within us. Have faith in your inner power, you will get rid of fear.

"I will fear no evil;
For thou art with me."
Psalm 23:4

"I sought the Lord
And He heard me
And delivered me
From all my fears."
Psalm 34:4

Don't become panicky when fear strikes. Calm down and relax. Learn to smile in the face of fear. The situation may not be as bad as you think and may be necessary for your growth. Take a more objective view and change your perception of the situation that upsets you and triggers fear. Analyze your fear. What is it? Where did it come from? Learn everything there is to know about the situation. Finding the root of your problem will help to solve your problem and give you a new life full of confidence in yourself and in your skill. Pray and ask for divine guidance. Nothing can frighten you because God is with you all the time. He is your best friend. You belong to Him and He will protect you.

"God takes up all the burdens
And the care of His devotees
Who worship Him
And meditate upon Him
With an undistracted mind
God brings attainment
Of what His devotees have not
And security in what they have."
The Gita 9:22

Don't run away from fear. Face it and bring it to light. Only by facing fear we can be creative and find solutions to our problems.

Don't be haunted by the fear of death. Death comes when you cease to learn and grow. Death is the reality of impermanence of existence. It is inevitable for the one who is born.

Death is certain to one
That is born
And birth is certain
That has died.
Therefore you should not mourn
For what is unavoidable."
The Gita 2:27

Death is a transition phase of eternal life. It renews life to
another dimension like abandoning old clothes and putting on
new ones.

> *"As leaving aside worn-out garments*
> *People acquire new ones.*
> *So leaving aside worn-out bodies*
> *A new body is taken*
> *By the Spirit within."*
>
> The Gita 2:22

> *"As a goldsmith, taking a piece of gold, turns it into another, newer,*
> *and more beautiful shape, even so does the Self after throwing away*
> *this body and dispelled its ignorance, make unto himself another, newer*
> *and more beautiful shape like that of the gods."*
>
> Brihadaranyak Upanishad 4:4:4

> *"God hath given to us eternal life,*
> *And this life is in His Son*
> *He that hath the Son hath life:*
> *And he that hath not the Son of God hath not life."*
>
> 1 John 5:11 and 12

Life is an expression of a timeless, changeless Spirit which
was never born, will not grow old and will never die.

> *"The body is mortal*
> *But the changeless Spirit within*
> *Is immortal.*
> *It pervades the universe*
> *And is indestructible*
> *No one has the power*
> *To change the changeless."*
>
> The Gita 2:17

Death is a great teacher. It tells us that we are not here
forever. Your existence is limited. So waste no time. Love all

and contribute to the welfare of humanity. Awareness of our mortality gives us understanding of the value of earthly possessions, brings us face to face with the Reality of life and enriches our stay on earth. So death need not be viewed fearfully.

The experience of overcoming fear will bring new confidence in yourself to face the demanding situations of life as a challenge rather than a threat. You will realize that your experience is nothing but a test of your spiritual growth and freedom. This experience will enhance your love of God and extend it to the love of all the creatures in the being of God. God will be seen in all and adored. To see God in the world and world in God is to fear nothing and hate no one.

Depend only on the Lord. Give yourself fully to Him. This is all that is needed for the Divine to lead you to a blissful life free from fear, worry, sorrow, and pain.

"He that dwelleth
In the secret place
Of the most High
Shall abide
Under the shadow
Of the Almighty."
Psalm 91:1

"Cast all your care upon Him
Because He cares for you."
1 Peter 5:7

Love and Relationships

Good relationships are the very foundation of a happy and joyful living. A loving relationship is blameless and free from exploitation and expectation. Developing a healthy relationship within the framework of our present way of living is a tremendous challenge to every one of us. The difficulty to create a healthy relationship comes when we separate human and spiritual and face the contradiction of the two realities we live in—the outer and the inner Reality. The best way to develop a desired relationship is to harmonize the two realities by performing the duties of life with the principles of the inner Truth. This means taking a trip to the spiritual domain of the inner world to explore who we really are. Healthy relationships must have a solid spiritual foundation to develop faith, wisdom, courage, understanding and compassion. These qualities are needed to open our hearts to human beings and to God, to weave together the realities of the outer and the inner life and counteract the divisive forces that block the flow of love and destroy a healthy relationship.

Personal relationships cannot be based just on fulfilling your own needs without being sensitive and supportive of the needs of others around you. You cannot blame any one for a relationship that has gone sour; nor can you try to have another person fit into the fantasy version of the ideal partner you are looking for. You pave a negative path in your life with your own hands. Develop a healthy and loving relationship by a way of living that controls and conditions your mind and ego.

Ego—the distorted image of our life—is a misunderstanding of what we truly are. Ego is a very powerful force, and if we allow, it may dominate our entire lives and manipulate our thoughts, feelings and emotions and distort our perceptions according to its selfish whims. Ego forces us to believe that we are right and others are at fault. When one becomes a slave of the ego, he thinks he is the master of all things and beings and he sinks down to the lowest level of selfishness. In the name of love, he projects his ego in his dealings with others and unknowingly chokes a good relationship that soon comes to an end. The ego standing between our personal self and the real Self is the main obstacle to our growth. It is almost impossible to erase ego, but it can be controlled by the practice of spiritual disciplines. By control over our ego we gain a very powerful force to enjoy a loving relationship. We feel that we are part of the whole—one with others—and realize that separate identity is an illusion.

Another important factor in developing a healthy relationship is communication. Unfortunately, many of us are not conversant with the art of communication. How many times have you thought of one thing and said another? Poor or faulty communication often leads to misunderstanding and misinterpretation of what you really mean.

Communication is not just speech and articulation. In a healthy communication you see another person from his or her frame of reference without judging or preaching. Hence the type of person you are, your conduct, your ability to listen and understand are critical for effective communication. Communication is the way to open our hearts and express our good feelings and compassion. Right communication eliminates the negative aspects and enhances the positive aspects of relationship and profoundly affects our emotional well-being. When the communication is based on love and understanding, it heals the wound and paves the path for reconciliation. So be polite in your conversation and be careful not to hurt anyone by your speech. Words we put in our conversation affect perception and understanding. By not using harsh words you will avoid conflict and have a satisfying relationship.

> Love is the life of a lasting relationship
>> That grows through your commitment and caring
> Give and receive without attaching a string
>> And lay the foundation of a delightful living.
> If you want the relationship
>> To be intimate and exciting,
> Develop your communication skill

And love your partner without judgement
Poor faulty communication is often the cause
Of painful separation and misunderstanding
Inconsistencies in your speech and action
	Lead to misinterpretation of your innocent thinking.
To enlarge your finite relationship
And focus beyond each other
Go inside to know yourself
And embrace the blissful creator.

"Verily, not for the sake of the husband is the husband dear but a husband is dear for the sake of the Self. Verily, not for the sake of the wife is the wife dear but a wife is dear for the sake of the Self. Verily, not for the sake of the sons are the sons dear but the sons are dear for the sake of the Self."
Brihadaranyaka Upanishad 2:4:5

Love gives lessons of forbearance and patience and paves the path of reconciliation and forgiveness. By forgiveness we avoid pain, resolve anger, and relieve depression.

Forgiveness is the righteousness of the Infinite
Forgive others if you want God to forgive you
Forgiveness repairs the wrong you have done,
	Put things right and allow your growth to continue.

Forgiveness is a sign of maturity, wisdom, and compassion that brings joy, peace, and laughter to life. Forgiveness does not consist in thinking ourselves morally superior to others; nor does it indicate an act of cowardice or an excuse to put up with a person you do not like. Forgiveness cannot be forced, it comes from the depth of love within.

Forgiveness is the core of all religions
And comes from the sweetness of love
Forgive those you have not forgiven yet
And receive the divine blessing from above.

> *"And when ye stand praying, forgive,*
> *If ye have ought against any:*
> *That your Father also which is in heaven*
> *May forgive you your trespasses.*
> *But if ye do not forgive*
> *Neither will your Father which is in heaven*
> *Forgive your trespasses."*
>
> St. Mark 11:25 and 26

Forgiveness provides an opportunity to rise above ego and see things in their true perspective beyond their physical appearances and change our opinion to judge others. The moment we forgive, we experience the connectedness of all beings and correct our misconception that we are separate. We realize that forgiveness is a necessary virtue to attain peace of mind.

> Forgiveness goes beyond ego
> Erases fear, anger, and depression
> It reconciles differences
> With lots of love and compassion.
> When forgiveness takes us above imperfections
> We touch the essence of beings
> And feel the wholeness of life
> From this awareness of all things.
> No doubt that this world
> Would be a better place for living
> If we put love in action
> And manifest the act of forgiving.

We progress on the path of perfection when we love and forgive others. Don't blame God for the situation you are in. Your ignorance has brought the delusion.

> *"Do not say*
> *God gave you this delusion*
> *It is the ignorance of your own nature*

That gives you this delusion.
Although the Lord is everywhere
He does not partake
In the good or evil deeds of any person
The Divine is the light of infinite knowledge
When the knowledge is covered
By the darkness of ignorance
Then our judgement is deluded."
The Gita 5:14 and 15

Don't hold any grievance or resentment towards any person.
Give up the idea of vengeance. Don't try to get even with people
you think have hurt you. Holding a grudge or trying to get even
will imprison your mind, thwart your growth, and increase your
anger and pain. Only forgiveness can bring an end to this vicious
cycle.

"Therefore, as God's chosen people,
Holy and dearly loved,
Clothe yourself with compassion
Kindness, humility, gentleness, and patience.
Bear with each other and forgive
Whatever grievances you may have
Against one another.
Forgive as the Lord forgave you."
Colossians 3:12 and 13

Today psychologists and therapists are beginning to
understand that forgiving is not only a theological concept of
the religious domain but also an important aspect of human
existence. It releases negative thoughts of bitterness and
resentment, transforms the mind and reaches out to heal the
breaches in a relationship.

Change your perception and response, the world will be
yours. Try always to fill the mind with loving and peaceful
feelings towards all. You are not a product of the past. You are
the embodiment of joy of the present. When we live in the

present, we forget the past and our capacity to forgive increases. Surrender the past and the future in the hands of the Lord. Make the present moment joyful by the feeling of love for those you have not forgiven yet. Find a way to forgive them and don't expect any return for your noble act of forgiveness.

"Let all bitterness
And wrath and anger
And clamor, and evil speaking
Be put away from you
With all malice.
And be ye kind one to another
Tender hearted,
Forgiving one another
Even as God for Christ's sake
Hath forgiven you."
Ephesians 4:31 and 32

Service

Service is life. Make a better life by serving others. There are various ways to serve people. There is no such thing as great or small service. All services are noble and provide us an opportunity to grow.

We are here on earth
>   To love serve and be useful to each other
Needs of people are many
>   Hence the ways to serve are large in number.
You may teach people to read and write
>   To erase their prejudice and ignorance
People will then know how best to serve life
>   With great zeal and self-confidence.
Always help the weak and the sick
>   To bring a smile on their face
You will get a great satisfaction
>   And will be rewarded by the divine Grace.
You can donate your money
>   To help the victims of a natural disaster
Or create a trust fund
>   To assist those whose financial needs are greater.
You can enlighten the people around you
>   And erase their spiritual blindness
It will help them
>   To manifest their inner strength, beauty and goodness.

True spiritual practice brings a genuine understanding of the underlying interconnectedness of all beings by uplifting our inner consciousness and at the same time manifesting that consciousness over here on earth. In other words it brings prayer, love, and meditation out into the world around us and manifests it as caring and serving. It is possible to harmonize the inner and outer aspects of our existence and develop the motive of selfless service by increasing our awareness of the sorrows and pains of others and honestly looking for the solution within ourselves.

"Love ye your enemies,
And do good,
And lend
Hoping for nothing.
Be ye merciful
As your Father also is merciful."
St. Luke 6:35 and 36

The eternal flow of love is sustained by the divine act of giving. The sacred intention of this process balances the polarities of existences and brings peace and harmony in life. If you want joy and happiness, serve others with what you cherish most.

Giving is the spirit of life
    Make a life by what you give
Give freely to the poor and the needy
    And let your mind thrive.
It is very difficult to give freely
    Without any interest or expectation
However, you can do it
    Expanding your vision with love and compassion.
Love is letting go
    Of your selfish desire for hoarding
And to open yourself
    To a joyful life of giving.
True giving is really receiving
    Always give more than you receive
Death comes when you stop giving
    So give freely to survive.
The joy of life comes from giving
    Not from earthly acquisition
So develop a detached attitude
    To give freely with great compassion.

True giving is non-egotistic and is free from the desire of name and fame. It is distinguished by the marks of unselfishness, love, and humility. If you stop giving, you block the flow of

64

love. Blocking the flow of love leads to stagnation. Stagnation means death. Giving is the best way to reach God in man and man in God. Because love of God is nothing but unconditional giving by beings of love.

"That gift which is made to one
From whom no return is expected,
With the feeling
That it is our duty and obligation
To give in proper place and time
To a worthy cause
Is held to be the best."
The Gita 18:20

Love and charity are different aspects of life. Life expands or shrinks in proportion to the act of giving. The more you give, the more you grow to be a better human being. Nothing is worth more than the joy and satisfaction that comes with the effort to fulfill the needs of some one else. The profound feeling of charity and the deep spiritual experience of oneness in love are the motivation of self sacrifice of many saints and sages to redeem the entire creation.

Charity is born of love and trust
One act of charity teaches more of God
Than all the books of theology.
Always be gracious to the poor
And serve the afflicted soul
You will know the universe
Without any schooling in cosmology.
When God comes at your door
As a ragged beggar
Lay down your treasure
And serve Him by your charity
Give with lots of love
To turn the world into a heaven
And pave the path
For your own prosperity.

"I stand at the door
And knock;
If any man hears my voice,
And opens the door,
I will come in to him,
And will sup with him.
And he with Me."

Revelation 3:20

St. Augustine summarized much about the meaning of charity when he said, *"Charity is a virtue which when our affections are perfectly ordered, unites us to God, for by it we love Him."*

"And now abideth faith, hope, charity
These three
But the greatest of these is charity."

1 Corinthians 13

To acquire the art of giving freely we must develop an attitude to give up the very things that we feel we need most and do not want to part with. Through our lives we progress by giving up our deepest attachments and unreal expectations. Giving up attachment bestows us the freedom and ability to discriminate between real and unreal, between what we need and what we want, between what we can change and what we cannot change, between necessities and luxuries of life.

"When a person
Loses attachment to sense objects
And to action,
When he renounces
Lust and all selfish desires
Then he climbs
To the highest point of spiritual discipline."

The Gita 6:4

Pointers to Make a Life
by Loving and Serving

Love is the Reality of Life
And the emblem of perfection and goodness
Love satisfies our inner needs
And takes us to higher levels of consciousness.
Love—the life of virtues
Inspires us to serve and give
Love removes fear and anger
Creating opportunities to forget and forgive.
Through love and service
Realize the oneness of creation
Awareness of unity
Will make you free from delusion.
To see with an equal eye
Love gives the lesson of equanimity
Sorrow and joy then becomes one
Due to the knowledge of equality.
Human love and relationships cannot grow
Without a solid spiritual foundation
So, follow the moral laws
And the spiritual rules and regulations.
Life is precious, life is holy,
Life is divine beauty
Keep it that way
With love and service to humanity.

"For this is the message
That ye heard from the beginning;
That we should love one another."
1 John 3:11

Persistently practice the following principles to achieve a satisfying and meaningful life.
1. Love is the creative and transformative power of the

universe. Through unconditional love perceive others as the reflection of your own being and touch the essence of being human.

2. Extend love and get control of your mind to acquire the virtue of equanimity. You will tackle the adverse situations better with patience and understanding. You will not be a victim of ego and selfish desire.

3. Don't judge and criticize people. See the goodness and strength of others and overlook their imperfections and weaknesses. Judgement blinds us. Love restores the sight and takes us beyond fear and worry.

4. Fear and worry are not real. They are creations of an ignorant mind. A disciplined mind can counteract the gloomy feelings of fear and worry by entertaining noble thoughts of love and compassion.

5. The best antidote to fear and worry is the awareness of the infinite strength, wisdom, and bliss within us. Have faith in your inner power, you will get rid of fear.

6. Don't run away from fear. Face it and analyze it. Finding the root of the problem you can be creative and find solution to your problem.

7. Don't be haunted by the fear of death. Death comes when you cease to learn and grow. Death is the reality of impermanence of existence. Awareness of our mortality gives us understanding of the value of earthly possessions, brings us face to face with the reality of life and enriches our stay on earth. So death need not be viewed fearfully.

8. Pray and ask for divine guidance. Give yourself fully to Him. Nothing can frighten you because God is with you all the time. He is your best friend. You belong to Him. He will protect you and lead you to a blissful life free from fear, worry, sorrow, and pain.

9. Develop your communication skills. You will enjoy a loving relationship. In a healthy communication you see another person from his or her frame of reference without judging or preaching, and open your heart and express your good feeling and compassion. This will eliminate the negative aspects and

enhance the positive aspects of relationships.

10. Love gives lessons of forbearance and patience and paves the path of reconciliation and forgiveness. By forgiving you avoid pain, resolve anger and relieve depression. Don't hold any grievance or resentment toward any person. Holding a grudge or trying to get even will imprison your mind, thwart your growth, and increase your anger and pain. Only forgiveness can bring an end to this vicious cycle.

11. Service is life. Make a better life by serving others. There is no such thing as great or small service. All services are noble and provide us an opportunity to grow.

12. Eternal flow of love is sustained by the divine acts of giving and charity. The more you give, the more you grow into a better human being. To acquire the art of giving freely you must develop an attitude to give up the very things that you feel you need most and do not want to part with.

"Whosoever has my commands and obeys them,
He is the one who loves Me.
He who love me will be loved by my Father
And I too will love him
And show myself to him."

John 14:21

69

IV
Pay Attention and Live the Present

*"This is the day
Which the lord hath made:
We will rejoice and be glad in it."*
Psalms 118:24

Do not brood over
    The happenings of yesterday
Treasure the experience
    Of what is history today.
Dreaming all the time
    Of a magical life tomorrow
The present then passes by
    Leaving a lot of sorrow.
Paying attention is to calm the mind
    And be one with your surrounding
Then you see things the way they are
    And get the real understanding.
Focus your attention on one thing at a time
    And filter out distracting thought
You will then unwind and relax
    In the joy and peace it would impart.
To experience the magic of the nowness
    Pay attention to what is right here
The present is potent with opportunities
    To love others and get rid of fear.
Paying attention and living the present
    We reach the state of non-duality
Where you and I become one
    And merge with the ultimate Reality.

Paying Attention

Paying attention means to merge completely with what you are doing, seeing, hearing, or feeling now without any distraction or reservation. Total oneness with what is going on now—no matter good or bad—is the most natural way to experience life fully, relieve pain, and discover the peace you were looking for. Unfortunately, many times we fail to pay attention because we want what is pleasant to us. In the name of good life, safety, and security, we are trying to create a world according to our liking by filtering out the things we do not like. As a result, we never see things the way they really are and totally miss the greatest pleasure of just being here right now. Don't dream away your precious life hoping for a better tomorrow. That tomorrow may never come. Don't be preoccupied with what has already happened. Otherwise you will be constantly drifting away from what you truly are, from the delight of your being.

In paying attention you avoid unnecessary value judgements and impose preferences on the situations. You learn to accept and experience the situation as it is without complaining or blaming anyone. You take the responsibility for your own life and need not convince others of your point of view. You consider every aspect of life as equally important and precious. You become detached, carefree and to some extent timeless. You learn to see things in their true perspective with an equal eye and experience the wholeness of life in a more loving and meaningful way.

Living the present is living the true spirituality which is not at odds with the life in the world. True spirituality brings harmony between the inner and outer world and reveals the sacred in the most ordinary happening of everyday life.

Yogas for Paying Attention

We cannot force ourselves to become one with what is happening now. It is a spontaneous and effortless process. We pay attention when the mind withdraws from all thoughts except the one to which it is subjected, without interruption, for a long time. We can develop and intensify our ability to be in oneness with the happenings of this very moment by four ways. These are called Yogas. Yogas are very powerful, potent methods for inner transformation, growth, and self-discovery. There are four Yogas, depending on the four tendencies of the mind. The four Yogas are:

1. Jnana-Yoga: the way of knowledge.
2. Bhakti-Yoga: the way of love and devotion.
3. Karma-Yoga: the way of selfless service.
4. Raja-Yoga: the way of concentration and meditation.

In all these Yogas the mind attains one-pointed awareness focused only on the present, since in this awareness there is neither past nor future, but just the present moment.

1. Jnana-Yoga

The knowledge of the One, from whom emanates a never ending procession of varied existences and in whom and by whom they exist is called the Jnana-Yoga. Jnana-Yoga gives the knowledge and wisdom to pay attention and be one with the present moment.

> *"I am the origin of all*
> *From Me all comes forth*
> *The wise know this*
> *And worship Me with all their heart."*
> The Gita 10:8

74

There are two kinds of knowledge—lower knowledge (Apara Vidya) and higher knowledge (Para Vidya). Lower knowledge is the knowledge of the manifested universe and is limited by the parameters of time and space. Scientific knowledge is lower knowledge. Lower knowledge can be gained by bits and pieces through human intellect and sensual perception. Hence, it is inferential, conceptual, and can be expressed in words. In this knowledge, there is a split between the knower and the known.

The higher knowledge (Para Vidya) is that by which one knows the Self (Atman) and the Supreme Consciousness (Brahman). It is a nonintellectual experience of the way the universe is in its reality, and transcends all sensual perception. This knowledge is infinite—no beginning and no end. In this knowledge there is no differentiation between the thinker and the thought, the subject, and the object. Hence, this knowledge cannot be expressed verbally and defies all conventional ways of knowing.

"By means of higher knowledge, the wise beholds every where the changeless Reality—which transcends the senses, which is uncaused, which is indefinable, which is all pervading and subtler than the subtlest, which is everlasting and is the source of all things and beings."
The Mundaka Upanishad 1:1:6

The power behind every activity of nature and human being is the Supreme Absolute Spirit. Neither by senses nor by intellectual reasoning can the Supreme Spirit be comprehended. By spiritual practice when the ego and the senses die down, the Truth of the Absolute is revealed. By this revelation one achieves victory over death and that becomes immortal. The followers of the path of Jnana know that life is an expression of this timeless and changeless Supreme Spirit. Death is the entrance gate to a new experience of the never ending process of evolution of the eternal life.

"The Self—the Immortal Spirit—behind every activity of human

being resides in the heart of all beings. He who makes himself free from selfish desire and the cravings of the senses, beholds the greatness of the Spirit through the tranquility of the mind."

The Katha Upanishad 1:2:20

"Having realized the Self, which is birthless, intangible, formless, undecaying, eternal, everlasting, and without beginning or end, one achieves victory over death and becomes immortal."

The Katha Upanishad 1:3:15

The path of Jnana requires a strong sense of discrimination. It is suited only to those who are of philosophical nature with a keenly analytical mind and an intensely powerful will.

"In the pursuit of a Truth, a person should discriminate between good and pleasant. He who chooses the good attains happiness. He who prefers the pleasant, misses the goal."

The Katha Upanishad 1:2:1

"Ignorance is destroyed by awakening to knowledge. The experiencer then advances toward the highest."

Patanjali's Yoga Sutras II:26 and 27

2. Bhakti-Yoga

The single-minded devotion to the Supreme is Bhakti Yoga —the Yoga of love, adoration, and devotion. This path is suited to most people because love is the essence of every being. By following the path of Bhakti the mind becomes one-pointed and can effortlessly pay attention to the present.

*"Those whose minds are fixed on Me
Revere Me with steadfast love
And worship Me with absolute faith
They have the perfect understanding of Bhakti."*

The Gita 12:2

"Fix thy mind on Me alone
Make thy understanding enter into Me
And thou shalt dwell in Me
Of this there is no doubt."
The Gita 12:8

Absolute devotion is not possible unless one conquers and controls the mind so that personal egotism and selfish desire are burned up and the mind becomes one pointed. By conquering the mind one becomes equal minded and touches the Inmost Truth from which flows love, joy, and peace.

"Keeping the mind even
In happiness and misery,
Gain and loss,
Victory and defeat,
Then get ready for life's struggle
And you will not commit any sin."
The Gita 2:38

The characteristics of a person living the present:

"He is pure, untroubled
And able to deal with the unexpected.
He has no expectation
And he is unconcerned
About the result of his actions.
He neither delights in what is pleasant
Nor does he dread what is unpleasant
He neither grieves nor craves.
His attitude is the same
Toward friend and foe,
Good and evil.
He is free from attachment,
And indifferent to honor and insult,
Heat and cold
pleasure and pain.

To him blame and praise are equal,
He has control over his speech and anger,
He is content with whatever he gets
He has no fixed abode.
His mind is fixed upon Me
And his heart is full of devotion."

The Gita 12:16 - 19

3. Karma-Yoga

Finding the Reality through selfless work. The basic requirements, to pay attention and selfless work, are the same viz transcendence of ego and personal desire. Every action has a reaction. We get caught up in the reaction of our action because we always expect a return. This is the cause of frustration and misery. When the consciousness is lifted through knowledge, love and devotion beyond all attachments, ego and selfish desire then all actions proceed from the Inner Spiritual Power and become dedicated worship for union with the indwelling divine Spirit.

"The world is imprisoned in selfish action,
Except when actions are performed
As worship of God,
Therefore you must perform every action sacramentally
And be free from all attachments to results."

The Gita 3:9

"The goal of wisdom and the goal of service
Are the same
The ignorant one fails to see
That knowledge and action are one."

The Gita 5:5

Karma-Yoga is really a devotional approach to attaining perfection through the performance of work as worship. This change in attitude through spiritual discipline reveals the secret of how to work freely without being bound to it. The desireless work without any egotistic motive or attachment leads to a calm equality and peaceful state of mind that is not perturbed by sorrow and pain. The work ceases to be ours when we realize that we are not the real doers of work but are only passive instruments of the will of God. This makes all actions a means of inner spiritual rebirth—a gateway to freedom and not bondage.

> *"Shake off the fever of ignorance*
> *Stop hoping for return*
> *Fix your mind on the indwelling Spirit*
> *Be free from the sense of ego.*
> *Dedicate all your actions to Me*
> *Then go forward and fight."*
>
> The Gita 3:30

Living in the Inner Spiritual Truth, do all works, not as yours but as His working through you, and be free from the limitations of ignorance and imperfections. Karma-Yoga shows how unattached selfless work perfects the means to pay attention and make the world a heaven.

> *"The blazing fire turns wood to ashes*
> *The fire of knowledge turns to ashes*
> *All selfish attachment to work.*
> *On earth there is no purifier*
> *As great as this spiritual wisdom*
> *When a person is made perfect in Yoga*
> *He knows its truth within his heart."*
>
> The Gita 4:37 and 38

4. Raja-Yoga

A practical and scientifically worked out method to manifest the Divinity within by psychic control. By controlling and concentrating the mind one gains profound knowledge of the One out of which emanates the diversity of the manifested universe. Raga-Yoga takes us to the infinite ocean of knowledge and power within us and provides self-confidence to take responsibility for our own lives and actions. When the mind becomes focused through the practice of Raja-Yoga, paying attention becomes spontaneous and effortless.

There are, of course, some preconditions for the practice and effectiveness of this yoga.

You must feel a strong urge to lift your consciousness and change for the better. Do not get discouraged by your failure or mistakes. Have courage and faith in yourself. Learn from the mistake and go ahead with your life.

"Sickness, mental laziness, doubt, lack of enthusiasm, sloth, craving for sense-pleasure, false perception, despair caused by failure to concentrate and unsteadiness in concentrations: these distractions are the obstacles to yoga."

The Patanjali's Yoga Sutras 1:30

You must make a firm commitment to be very regular in your practice. Your sincerity and regular practice are the key to your success. Just listening or reading about the Yoga is not of much help. You should have regular hours and a fixed place to practice Yoga. Keep a well ventilated room or a corner of your house that is free from noise for the practice. Always preserve the sacredness and purity of this place. Enter this place when you are perfectly clean in body and peaceful in mind. You can decorate the place with flowers and pictures that create an atmosphere of holiness. The best hours for practice are early morning, early evening and midnight.

Avoid undesirable company and be compassionate to those who are in distress. Always maintain a positive and happy attitude. You must also maintain good health. If you are not in good health, you cannot sit properly in the same posture for a long time and concentrate. A weak body and a weak mind cannot achieve success in Yoga. Eat a balanced diet, exercise regularly and get a periodic physical check up. However, do not be over obsessive with your health. Remember good health is only the means and not the goal of your mission. Avoid the extremes and follow the middle path.

"Yoga is not for the person who eats too much or who fasts excessively. It is not for him who sleeps too much or sleeps too little. The person who has learned to be moderate in sleeping, eating, working, and recreation will come to the end of sorrow."

The Gita 6: 16 and 17

Steps of Raja-Yoga

There are eight steps in Raja-Yoga.

The first step is Yama. It is the practice of truthfulness and abstention from harming others. Our speech and thoughts must be truthful always in conformity with our action. The practice of truthfulness and abstention from harming others means cultivating love which leads to the awareness of our connectedness and the unity behind the diversity.

"The obstacles of Yoga—such as acts of violence and untruth— may be directly created or indirectly caused, they may be motivated by greed, anger or self-interest, they may be small or moderate or great but they always bring pain and sorrow."

The Patanjali's Yoga Sutras 11:34, 35 and 36

The second step is Niyama. It is the practice of the cleanliness of the body, purity of the mind, and contentment. Yama and Niyama are really moral training and cultivation of ethical values. Without this training and understanding of the moral values we cannot concentrate and progress in Yoga.

"As a result of the purity of the heart comes the cheerfulness of the mind, the power of concentration, control of the passions and the fitness for the vision of who we really are.
"As a result of contentment, one gains supreme happiness."

The Patanjali's Yoga Sutras II:41 and 42

The third step is Asana or Posture. The posture is to be seated in a position which is firm but relaxed. It enables you to

81

sit comfortably with the minimum expenditure of energy and meditate for a long time.

"The posture becomes firm and relaxed through control of the natural tendencies of the body and through meditation on the Infinite."
The Patanjali's Yoga Sutras II:47

You can sit on a chair or on the floor. Perfection of Yoga is not affected by it. If you sit on a chair, put the feet under the chair. It is necessary for the posture to keep the spinal column erect, holding the chest, neck, and head in a straight line. In the most natural posture all internal organs function in harmony without any interference from outside.

If you are able to sit on the floor, try the posture known as "Padmasana"—the posture of the lotus—with legs crossed, soles upward with feet resting on the thighs. The hands rest upon the lap, the left over the right with palms inward and thumbs touching one another. If you sit in this posture, the body will automatically be held erect and give a feeling of firmness of being part of the ground.

"Placing the body in a straight posture
With chest, the throat and the head held erect
Causing the senses and the mind
To enter into the heart
The wise crosses all the fearful currents
By means of the raft of the Supreme."
The Shvetashvatara Upanishad 11:8

"Hold your body, head and neck firmly
In a straight line
And keep your eyes from wandering
And the vision indrawn
As if gazing at the tip of the nose."
The Gita 6:13

Relax and do the following exercises. Repeat each exercise three times and bring the head back to erect position after each exercise.

a. Bow the head slowly forward till the chin touches the chest. Then softly lean backward till the head rests on the spine.

b. Slowly twist the head right as far as possible. In the same way twist it to the left.

c. Roll the head slowly clockwise in a wide circle. Repeat the same process in a counter clockwise direction.

The fourth step is Pranayama. Pranayama is the knowledge and control of Prana—the vital energy that sustains life. The functions of the mind and the senses are expressions of the force of Prana. There is only one Prana that pervades the whole universe. By the knowledge of Prana we know every thing.

We draw Prana from the universe by breathing. So breath may be considered a manifestation of Prana. By controlling the breath we get control over Prana. The person who has controlled Prana has conquered not only his or her own mind and senses but also the mind and the senses of all beings of the universe. By controlling Prana one gains gigantic will power and develops a tremendous magnetic personality that attracts thousands of people towards him or her.

According to Yoga philosophy there are seven centers of consciousness starting from Muladhara at the base of the spine to the highest center Sahasrara at the top of the head. These centers, also called "Lotuses," are shown here.

According to Raja-Yoga a huge reservoir of vital energy called the "Kundalini" is situated at the base of the spine. When the Kundalini is aroused it travels up the spine producing various degrees of enlightenment. Traveling all the way

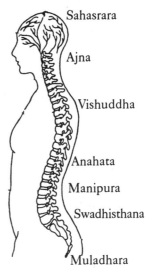

Sahasrara

Ajna

Vishuddha

Anahata

Manipura

Swadhisthana

Muladhara

83

up, it reaches the top most center Sahasrara and merges with the highest non-dual state of Supreme consciousness, Samadhi —the state of profound peace and bliss where there is no longer the dualism of the knower and the known.

The main purpose of breathing exercises is to control Prana and thereby calm the mind and the senses so that they do not interfere with the prime objective—awakening Kundalini by meditation. There are various breathing exercises. Some of them are complicated and may be injurious to health if not done properly. Kundalini is a very potent power and is not something to be taken lightly.

Here is a harmless breathing exercise which may be used to calm the mind prior to meditation.

Close the right nostril with the thumb of the right hand and inhale slowly and gently through the left nostril to fill the lungs. Concentrate the mind on the feeling of inhaling pure and sacred Prana and sending a message to awaken Kundalini at the base of the spine. Hold the breath for a moment, closing the left nostril by pressing gently with the middle finger of the right hand. When you are doing that repeat the sacred syllable "OM." Release the right nostril and exhale slowly and gently through the right nostril. Feel as if you are expelling all the impurities from your body. Then still keeping the left nostril closed, inhale through the right nostril. Reverse the process and observe the whole process with great concentration. This observation will bring your mind to merge with what is happening at that moment and give you a greater sense of control over your life.

The fifth step is Pratyahara, withdrawing the mind from the sense objects.

"When the mind is withdrawn from sense objects, the sense organs also withdraw themselves from their respective objects and thus are said to imitate the mind. This is known a Pratyahara.
"Thence arises complete mastery over the senses."
The Patanjali's Yoga Sutras II:54 and 55

As long as there is desire in the mind the sense organs will move eagerly toward the objects of desire and drag the mind along with them.

"Pleasure conceived in the world of the senses
Have a beginning and an end
And give birth to misery.
The wise do not look for happiness in them."
The Gita 5:22

So the mind needs to be controlled to withdraw it from sense objects. When the mind becomes strong and self-controlled, the sense organs become its obedient servants. The best way to withdraw the mind from sense objects is to spend some time each day just watching the activities of the mind. Be very patient. Give it freedom to roam and think. You will be surprised to find that being watched in this way the mind gradually grows calmer and comes under your perfect control.

"Those who overcome the impulses of lust and anger,
Which arise in the body,
Make connection with the Inner Being
They live in joy.
They find their joy, their rest and their light
Completely within themselves
They live in freedom
And become united with the Lord.
Those who rise above selfish desire and anger
Through constant effort and determination
Conquer themselves
And gain control over passion and mind.
They experience the Self
And live forever in Nirvana."
The Gita 5:23, 24, and 26

"Holding the mind from restless roaming,
With his heart serene and firm dispassion,
A person finds complete fulfillment in Me.
In this state all fears
Dissolve in My peace and oneness.
And all actions proceed toward Me."
The Gita 6:14

"Then he knows that abiding joy
Can be realized only by a stilled mind
And not by the pleasure of the senses.
He stands firm in this faith.
Because of it he never wanders
From the innermost truth that all life is one
He counts none higher than this state
Because his faith is so certain
He cannot be shaken by heaviest sorrow."
The Gita 6:21 and 22

The first five steps are only a kind of training to prepare one for the next three very important steps of Raja-Yoga.

The sixth step is Dharana, concentrating the mind on one idea or object or on a spot inside or outside the body. You can hold the mind on any center of consciousness or fix it on your chosen ideal. By fixing the mind on one spot or idea you shut it off from inside and outside distractions.

Don't jump from one idea to another. Stick to one idea at a time and fix your whole mind on it. Think of it, dream of it, and let your whole mind and body be immersed in that one idea without any thought of time or the result. This concentration will lead you to a greater ability to make you fit for meditation which is really the breaking of contact with pain.

"For even an aspirant
Who abstains from sense pleasure
The stormy senses can drag him from the path
But they live in wisdom

86

Who subdue the senses
And keep their mind ever absorbed
And fixed only on Me."

The Gita 2:60 and 61

"He who is free from delusion
And whose mind and heart are fixed on Me
And knows Me as the Supreme Reality
Knows all that are to be known."

The Gita 15:19

The **seventh step is Dhyana,** unbroken thought toward the object of concentration. This prolonged and persistent concentration makes the mind one-pointed. This technique of making the mind one-pointed is called meditation. In meditation you receive direct knowledge and see things in the truth of their own nature, free from the distortion of the mind.

"The practice through which
A person learns to withdraw the mind
From selfish cravings
To the Self within
And thus attains union with the Lord
Is called meditation."

The Gita 6:18

"Controlling the body and the mind
One should practice meditation
To enjoy a healthy and meaningful life
Free from expectations
And attachment to material possession."

The Gita 6:10

Meditation begins with the concentration on the gross object. As the meditation progresses the mind gradually perceives the finer and finer states till the meditation becomes objectless or formless. This is the state where you become timeless and merge with the essence of existence. This state of knowledge and bliss can be achieved here while living.

> *"If a person has known It here*
> *Then there is truth;*
> *If a person has not known It here,*
> *There is great loss.*
> *Experiencing this Truth*
> *The wise becomes immortal."*
>
> The Kena Upanishad 2:5

The practice of meditation has been around us for thousands of years. It has been practiced in various forms; but the ultimate aim of all the forms is the same—to tap into the vast unexplored region of life, to know ourselves and enhance the joy of living. We cannot run away from the pains and problems of life. Meditation empowers us to counteract negative thoughts, depression, and feelings of emptiness. Through meditation, when the mind quiets down, we begin to experience a sense of inner calmness, contentment, and lasting happiness. Meditation is thus a very valuable tool to help you enjoy not only a longer but also a better life.

> *"The practice of meditation frees one*
> *From all afflictions.*
> *This is the path you should follow*
> *With determination and sustained enthusiasm."*
>
> The Gita 6:23
>
> *"When one constantly controls the mind and the senses*
> *Through the practice of meditation*
> *And seek the Divinity within*
> *He attains Nirvana,*
> *The state of abiding joy and peace in Me."*
>
> The Gita 6:15

Meditate daily at the same time and at the same place. There is no time limit. Begin with ten to fifteen minutes and gradually increase it. Early morning, noon, dusk, and midnight are good times for meditation. You can meditate any number of

times you like. Always end the meditation with a prayer of
happiness, and well-being to all.

"O! Supreme Lord, creator of the universe,
Embodiment of vital breath,
Destroyer of sin, pain and sorrow,
Bestower of Divine power and intellect,
Embodiment of peace and bliss.
Thou are the most effulgent,
Radiant, glorious, excellent and Supreme
We pray to Thee.
May Thou be propitious unto us.
Guide our intellect
And inspire us
To realize the oneness of the manifested universe.
O! Lord lead us
From the unrealities of the world
To the ultimate Reality
That propels the universe
Guide us from the darkness and chaos of ignorance
To the light and purity of knowledge
Lead us from mortality and limitations of the finite
To liberation, immortality and bliss of the Infinite.
OM, may everybody be happy
And free from disease and afflictions.
May everybody realize what is auspicious.
May everybody have good fortune,
And never face any adversity
Or suffer from misery.

Peace, peace, peace be unto us and peace and harmony be
everywhere and amongst all things and beings of the universe.

The eighth step is Absorption or Samadhi. Samadhi is
the state of super consciousness and can be attained by
intensifying dhyana or meditation. In this state you not only
get enlightenment, but you become it and know who you are
and unlock the mystery of life and death.

In this process of experiencing there is nothing to be grasped
as an object. There is also no one as a subject to grasp. In this

state of non-duality the mind no longer divides against itself and the differentiation between subject and object vanishes. Samadhi gives complete control of the thought waves of the mind. All mental distractions disappear and the mind becomes calm.

When the three fold processes—dharana, dhyana, and samadhi—are practiced assiduously on an object, one reaches the state called Sayama—the highest meditative state of existence.

These are the different methods to make the mind one-pointed for paying attention. Remember, practice is the key for first concentration upon an object and then continuing that concentrating for a length of time until the meditation becomes objectless and the true nature of the object shines forth.

Pointers to Pay Attention and Live the Present

Live the present and make it beautiful
Living the present is living with God
Past and future exist in dream
Present is the only gift from the Lord.
Concentration on one thing is meditation
It brings profound change in you
Meditation gives new vision and unveils wonders
That were hidden from view.
Blend your love and knowledge
To get ready for worldly action
Follow the eight steps of Raja-Yoga
For success in meditation.
Meditation is a spiritual fire that burns up
The thoughts that are harmful
Practice meditation to focus your attention
Only on one thought that is beautiful.

"When meditation is mastered,
The mind becomes unwavering
Like the flame of a lamp
That does not flicker
In a spot sheltered from wind."
The Gita 6:19

Persistently practice the following principles to achieve a satisfying and meaningful life.

1. Learn to merge completely with what you are doing, seeing, hearing, or feeling at this moment. Total oneness with the present is the most natural way to experience life fully, relieve pain, and get peace.

2. Don't dream away your precious life hoping for a better tomorrow. Don't be preoccupied also with what had already happened. Otherwise you will be drifting away from the delight of living.

3. Avoid unnecessary value judgements and try not to impose your liking or disliking on others. Learn to accept and experience a situation as it is without complaining or blaming any one.

4. Take the responsibility for your own life and consider every aspect of life as equally important and precious.

5. Be equal minded and compassionate to people and other living creatures.

6. Develop and intensify your ability to merge with the happenings of the present moment by following the Yogas prescribed here. By the practice of the Yogas your mind will attain one-pointed awareness focused only on the present, since in this awareness there is neither past nor future, but just the present.

7. Follow the steps of meditation one by one. Don't try to concentrate if you are not trained properly in ethical and moral values as described previously. You cannot do meditation unless you have mastered concentration. You cannot concentrate on the formless until you are able to concentrate on the gross object. You cannot go to the state of Samadhi until you have mastered meditation. Don't go too fast by making a short cut. A short cut of this type may be exceedingly dangerous.

A person becomes fit for meditation and can pay attention effortlessly.

> *"When the mind and the heart*
> *Are freed from delusion.*
> *When the steady will*
> *Has subdued the senses.*
> *When a person seeks solitude*
> *And is full of compassion.*
> *Eats but little*
> *Restrains speech, body and mind*
> *And devotes constantly to concentration*
> *And takes refuge in dispassion*
> *When the person casts away*
> *Vanity, violence, pride, lust, anger*

And becomes free from ego and selfishness
That person is ready to meditate
And pay attention."

The Gita 18:51, 52 and 53

V
Live Your Religion
and Take Refuge in God

"Praise Ye the Lord,
O give thanks unto the Lord:
For He is good:
For his mercy endureth forever."
Psalms 106:1

God is the Life of the cosmos
    He cannot be described by finite expressions
God resides in the bosom of every being
    And reveals Himself through noble actions.
God is past, present, and future
    And the only safety against a wrong turn
From God we come, by Him we exist
    And finally to Him we return.
Every human being is created with love
    In the image of God
We are expressions of the Life Eternal
    And instruments of the Lord.
God is existence as well as nonexistence
    And is beyond everything
Realize God and experience the supreme bliss
    of the Truth of His Being.
When we experience the profound plan
    Of unity behind the diversity
We realize God as a being
    Of infinite love and beauty.
Religion is the realization of the relationship
    Of humanity with the ultimate Reality
It is an inner awakening
    To an understanding of His immense creativity.
If you want to know
    The secret of a joyful living
Then live the virtues
    And always stay with your inner being.

When swami Vivekananda first visited Sri Ramakrishna at Dakshineswar he asked , *"Sir, have you seen God?"*

Without hesitation or doubt Sri Ramakrishna spontaneously replied, *"Yes, I have seen God. I see him as I see you here, only more clearly."*

These utterances are the expression of the depth of Sri Ramakrishna's inner spiritual identification with the Absolute. Through intellectual discursive reasoning, however subtle, it is not possible to see the invisible and communicate with Him. Only through the inner transformation does the possibility of finding God become a reality.

> *"Not by discourses*
> *Nor by intellectual analysis*
> *Nor through much scholarship*
> *Can God be attained*
> *By one who is without*
> *Strength, earnestness, knowledge, and detachment.*
> *If a person strives*
> *By means of his strong willpower,*
> *Devotion, knowledge, and renunciation*
> *His soul enters the abode of eternal bliss."*
> Mundaka Upanishad III.ii.3 and 4

The evolution of human consciousness that taps the inner power and gives birth to a new vision of our identity is a very slow process. But this spiritual awakening and gradual building of consciousness takes us from the state of multiplicity to the state where there is no duality. There is no split between the knower and the known. There cannot be any delusion or sorrow for a person who has reached this state which is the abode of our real Self—the Divinity within.

> *"Who knows all life*
> *As My manifestation*
> *And sees Me in all*
> *And all in Me*
> *He is never separated from Me."*
> The Gita 6:30

97

"The wise man who realizes all beings
As not distinct from his own Self
And his won Self
As the Self of all beings
Does not by virtue of that perception
Hates anyone
What delusion
What sorrow
Can there be
For that wise man
Who realizes the unity of all the existences
By perceiving all beings
As his own Self."

Isa Upanishad 6 and 7

To see one in many and many in one
    Is the life's mission
Then we know what we are
    And our link in the creation.
We are not separate
    But a joint family here
Love and harmony with all beings
    Will take us there.

Religion Is a Guide to Inner Transformation

Religion guides us through the process of evolution to experience the unity and the essence of being human. Through religion we realize our infinite potentiality and grow from where we are now to where we want to live in peace and harmony with others. Only religion—not science or philosophy—can fill this need.

God is Truth. Religion is love of God and hence a way of Truth. Truth is not the monopoly of any particular faith. Each religion has a characteristic feature of the universal Truth in its teachings of brotherhood, service, sacrifice, love, and compassion.

> *"All scripture is given by the inspiration of God,*
> *And is profitable for doctrine,*
> *For reproof, for correction*
> *For instruction in righteousness."*
> II Timothy 3:16

The apparent differences in the teachings of religion are, therefore, not contradictory. They complement each other. Religion thus offers a splendid opportunity to experience the interconnection and oneness of all things and beings. Only one religion—not others—will expand human consciousness and bring a life of hope without despair, pleasure without pain is a blasphemy.

All religions here have
One common mission
To see God and love
His delightful creation
Religion connects each one of us
With the same inner divinity
And shows that we belong
To a large family of humanity.

99

Understanding religion from this point of view will bring hope for a nobler life and lead to toleration, acceptance, peace, charity, love, and compassion. This will stop bloodshed and prevent cruelty that have been perpetuated in the name of religion.

The truest picture of religion is within our own experience of love, goodness, and happiness to all creatures. Who loves all beings and suffers the pain of every creature, he is fulfilling all the commandments of a religion. He is a true human being.

"When a person responds
To the joys and sorrows
Of every creature
As if they were his own
He or she attains the highest goal
Of a religious life."
The Gita 6:32

The fundamental Truth as taught by every religion is that man has to transform his lower nature and manifest the hidden Divinity within where lies the unity of the diverse existences. Live your religion to experience the highest level of human thought that goes beyond personal pleasure, profit or loss, success or failure, to a greater dimension of love, service and sacrifice.

"Not shaken by grief
Not elated by happiness
Free from fear,
Free from anger,
Free from the things of pleasure
Stable in mind and intellect
Is the religious seer."
The Gita 2:56

The goal of religion is to find God—the Reality of life. Without God life has no meaning. God is the creator, preserver, and destroyer, too, of this universe.

100

"I am the birth of the cosmos
Its dissolution too
I am He Who causes
Whatsoever exists
No other beside Me.
Upon Me the universe is held
Like heaps of pearls strung on a thread."
                                The Gita 7:6 and 7

"In His hand
Are the deep places of the earth
The strength of the hills
Is also His.
The sea is His
And He made it;
And His hands
Formed the dry land."
                                Psalm 95:4 and 5

God is so near, yet He seems so far. He is the light, but appears as darkness, as a void, as silence. This is the divine mystery. But the scriptures of different faiths and lands all echo in unison that in this darkness all light, in this void all fullness, and in this silence all delight are to be found in unlimited amount. We cannot find God if we do not strive hard to uplift our consciousness.

Through lots of love
      Prayer and intense meditation
You can meet the Spirit
      Of this wonderful creation.
To have a vision of God here on earth
      Follow the spiritual teachings
Develop a detached attitude
      As well as an equal mindedness to all beings.
The proof that you have
      Found God and real happiness
Is evident from your joy
      And the aura of godliness.

Take Refuge in God

To attain the goal of religious life we must take refuge in God. When we take refuge in God, the divine forces take hold of our lives and our problems and pains come to an end.

"God is our refuge and strength
A very present help in trouble."
Psalm 46:1

"In God is my salvation
And my glory
The rock of my strength
And my refuge
Is in God."
Psalm 62:7

"To Him alone you go for refuge
With whole being and heart.
By His grace supreme peace
And the eternal abode shall thou attain."
The Gita 18:62

"The Lord will give strength
Unto His people
The Lord will bless
His people with peace."
Psalm 29:11

Taking refuge in God means surrendering to Him completely. When one surrenders completely to God his personality, will and desire are no longer his but are taken by the Divine. It is God who then works in him and for him.

"It is God
Which worketh in you
Both to will
And to do His good pleasure."
Philippians 2:13

"From Whom emanates all existences
From Whom all things issue forth
And by Whom all the universe is pervaded
Worshipping verily Him
And offering all our actions to Him
A person attains perfection
And obtains eternal bliss."

The Gita 18:46

"Trust in the Lord
With all thine heart
And lean not
Unto thine own understanding.
In all thy ways
Acknowledge Him
And He shall direct thy path."

Proverb 3:5 and 6

When you take refuge in God, surrendering to Him completely, you overcome fear and worry. There is nothing to fear, nothing to worry about. You are under His protection. Nothing can touch you.

"Give Me your whole heart
Love and adore Me
Worship Me,
And revere Me always
And you shall find Me.
I promise this to you.
Because you are so dear to Me.
Abandoning all duties
Come to Me your sole refuge,
Fear no longer,
For I shall save you
From evils and bondage."

The Gita 18:65 and 66

"The Lord is my light
And my salvation
Whom shall I fear?
The Lord is the strength of my life
Of whom shall I be afraid?"
                                    Psalm 27:1

You can give yourself completely to God by a prayerful way of living. A prayerful way of living is a sincere dedication of the heart in which all we do—eating, drinking, working, resting, playing, or cooking—is done as an offering and worship to the glory of God and God alone.

"Whatever thou doest
Whatever thou eatest
Whatever thou offerest
Whatever thou givest away
Whatever doest thou for the Spirit
Do all those as an offering to Me."
                                    The Gita 9:27

"Blessed are they
That keep His testimonies
And that seek Him
With the whole heart."
                                    Psalm 119:2

Work as Worship

How many times have you heard, "I am too busy with my work and have no time to seek or worship God." This delusion comes when we separate Divinity from the activities of daily life and are dominated by the desire to get wealth, name, and fame through our work. We forget that we need to work not only to earn our living but also to get a better understanding of our very existence.

Work properly done not only satisfies
    Your physical needs and financial commitments
But also fills your inner void
    With the understanding of success and accomplishments.
Work properly done, called the unattached work
    Brings joy even when the going gets tougher
And provides wisdom for a better understanding
    And appreciation of our connectedness to each other.
Unattached work is pure
    And free from ego and selfish desire
It provides strength to overcome
    The temporary excitement of mundane pleasure.
Unattached work is not the goal of life
    But a means to find the ultimate Reality
Working this way you know who you really are
    And quickly return to the inner Divinity.

When you are obsessed by the demand of the fruit of your action and all your thoughts and feelings revolve around satisfying your desire, you are likely to miss the delightful aspects of life and may get frustrated and burnt out.

We are attached to our work by our ego and desire. Through our ego we think we are the doer and, guided by desire, we demand the fruit of our work. But if we rise above our normal mind, above our intellect by projecting ourselves into another level of awareness where personal ego and desire do not exist, the picture changes completely.

"Every action is performed by His will.
Whose soul is deluded
By his pride and egoism
He thinks, 'I am the doer!'
But he who has the true insight
Into the operations of nature
And its various functions
Does not demand the fruit of his actions
And does not get attached to his actions."
The Gita 3:27 and 28

By dissociating work from ego and desire, the work ceases to be ours and we no longer work for the fruit of the work but for the satisfaction of the real doer—the Supreme Lord. We become free and are able to act without being bound by its reactions—good or bad. Because at this state we do not work, it is the Divine within who acts, and we become an instrument of the Divine, but we still get the satisfaction that we long for.

"Abandoning the fruit of actions
The followers of the unattached action
Attains abiding peace.
The undisciplined
Attached to the fruit of action
Is a prisoner enslaved by action
And is never free."
The Gita 5: 12

"So do your duty,
But unattached ever,
By working without attachment
You reach the highest Truth and happiness."
The Gita 3: 19

By this non-attachment to work, all dualities—failure and success, victory and defeat—dissolve in the supreme tranquility of the perfect spiritual equality and all the reactions of our

106

activity are burned up in the purity of the Divine Knowledge. By offering credit and the fruit of the work to the Lord, the mind is liberated from the imprisonment of ignorance and imperfection. Work becomes a medium of love, a form of worship, and a practical means to achieve oneness with Him.

"You have the right to work
But never on its fruits
Let not the fruit of action be your motive
Never give way to inaction."

The Gita 2:47

"Perform every action
With your heart fixed on the Lord
Abandoning attachment
With an even mind
In success and failure."

The Gita 2:48

Prayer

Prayer is the most powerful force to shift the center of human consciousness and bring profound inner transformation. This awakening to the innermost Truth of the being is reflected in the outward changes of character, conduct and in the expanded vision of who we really are. Prayer needs no speech. He who prays fervently without any distraction does not think of the language or ritual of the prayer. He thinks only of God and keeps his heart immersed in divine love. Prayer is the most intimate and silent dialogue of love combined with utmost humility for friendship and union with the Spirit.

> Prayer is fellowship with God
> Through love's unique voice
> And see behind the darkness
> His wonderful smiling face.
> Prayer is love of God
> And His beautiful creation
> It uplifts the mind
> And brings profound transformation.
> God will always save you
> From worldly trouble and temptation
> If you pray to Him with love
> And utmost devotion.

When we direct all our attention and thought to the glory and adoration of God, the prayer becomes a living messenger of human virtues. It consecrates all our actions and leads us to the source of never-ending joy.

> *"With thoughts ever straying*
> *To no other objects*
> *Who thinks of Me constantly,*
> *For him I am easily attained."*
> The Gita 8:14

108

"Quickly I come to those
Who offer Me every action
And worship Me only
With unswerving devotion
Because they love Me
I save them
From sorrow and
The waves of the ocean of death."
The Gita 12:6 and 7

"And ye shall seek Me,
And find Me,
When Ye shall search for Me
With all your heart."
Jeremiah 29:13

"Fill your heart and mind with Me,
Make all your acts as an offering to Me
Bow down to Me in self—surrender.
If you set your heart upon Me thus
And take Me for your ideal
Above all others,
You will come to My being."
The Gita 9:34

"If you abide in me
And my words abide in you
Ye shall ask what ye will
And it should be done unto you."
John 15:7

Through prayer we grow from the state of separation to the state of oneness where everything and being are connected to God. By letting go of our idea of separation we see God in every creature and the whole creation in God. By this enlightenment we overcome selfishness, insecurity, and fear.

109

"Not hater of any living creature
Friendly and compassionate to all
Free from selfishness
And the delusion of 'I' and 'mine.'
Indifferent to pain and pleasure
Patient and forgiving
Who is ever content, self-controlled
And is of firm resolve,
Whose thoughts and consciousness
Are fixed on Me,
Who is devoted to Me
In intellect and in mind
Such a disciplined person is dear to Me."

The Gita 12:13 and 14

"When you have reached enlightenment
Ignorance will delude you no longer
In the light of your knowledge
You will see yourself in all creatures
And all creatures in Me."

The Gita 4:35

There is no special time or place for prayer. You pray at any place and at any time—morning, noon, evening, or night.

"From the rising of the sun
Unto the going down of the same
The Lord's name is to be praised."

Psalm 13:3

"I will sing unto the Lord
As long as I live
I will sing praise to my God
While I have my being."

Psalm 104:33

110

You can pray on a happy occasion as well as in adversity, when you cannot cope with life. When you feel that the things are not working the way they should and you see no hope in sight, that is the time to pray to God to guide you through the darkest night.

Help will come in a mysterious way through your prayer from sources that you thought far beyond the realm of possibility.

"And whatsoever ye shall ask
In my name,
That I will do."
John 14:13

" Whatever wish
People bring to Me in worship
That I grant them.
Whatever path people travel
Is My path.
No matter where they walk
It leads to Me."
The Gita 4:2

"Hear my prayer,
O Lord,
And let my cry come unto Thee.
Hide not thy face
From me in the day
When I am in trouble,
Incline thine ear unto me.
In the day
When I call,
Answer me speedily."
Psalm 102:1 and 2

To pray, sit in a comfortable position and relax. Be silent and think of going to the inner source of peace and bliss. Feel the profound sense of oneness and joy and pray.

> God give me strength
>   To get my work done
> To help the needy
>   And be useful to everyone.
> God give me knowledge
>   To enlighten those
> Who are immersed
>   In ignorance up to their nose.
> God give me vision
>   To see you every where
> And love all beings
>   Of your immense creation here.
> God give me faith
>   In your supreme power
> To overcome pains
>   And get rid of fear.
> God make me compassionate
>   To creatures big or small
> To comfort the sad
>   And bring joy to all.
> God have mercy on me
>   To serve and worship Thee
> To feel your presence
>   And your celestial beauty to see.

> *"Fill us at day break*
> *With your love,*
> *That all our days*
> *We may sing for joy."*
> Psalms 90:14

Pointers to Reach God

Everyone wants to be united with God
And get the divine guidance
Pass through the rugged road of spiritual life
And behold His Living Presence.
Treat with an equal eye birds and beasts
And every living creature
Respect all religious faiths
Because love and truth are their real feature.
Live your own religion
Close to the bone with devotion
To take refuge in God
And get out of delusion.
By practice bring the restless mind
In the silence of prayer and deep meditation
You will get the affirmation of God
And a profound feeling of holy sensation.
Give your whole heart
And the fruit of your action to God
That is the way to worship Him
And communicate with the Lord.
Celebrate each day
With praise to the glory of the Lord
You will experience a meaningful life
By the grace of God.

Persistently practice the following principles to achieve a satisfying and meaningful life.

1. Live your religion to experience the essence of being human. The religion offers a golden opportunity to realize the interconnectedness of all things and beings.

2. Love all beings and suffer the pain of every creature. You will fulfill all the commandments of a religion.

3. Transform your lower nature by following the spiritual disciplines and manifest the virtues within to experience the highest level of human thought that goes beyond personal

pleasure to a greater dimension of love, service and sacrifice.

4. Take refuge in God dedicating to Him your will and actions through prayer. Prayer is change, change is growth and growth is life. Make a meaningful life by your prayer. You will overcome problems of life, fear and anger.

5. Work freely with joy by making the ends and means the same. In other words make the work as a form of worship by rising above normal mind and intellect into another level of awareness where personal ego and desire do not exist.

6. Put your priorities in order. Become unattached and an instrument of the Divine, you will be free and bring blessings to yourself and to others.

7. Prayer is the most powerful force to shift the center of human consciousness and bring profound change for the better in your character and conduct. Prayer must be unselfish and is to be offered with great humility, devotion, love and compassion.

8. Keep your prayer simple. Prayer is not a speech to impress God. Prayer is for listening. We listen when we are quiet and observe silence—both inward and outward. God speaks through the silence of the prayer.

9. Pray at any place and at any time to experience your true nature. Pray together and stay together. When you feel that the going has become tough, pray to God to guide you through the darkest night.

> In the moments of trial
>   Always pray together and stay together
>   Pains and sufferings come and go
>   They never last forever.

10. Be patient and persistent. Increase your yearning to reach perfection and concern for others. You will reach the goal.

> *"Those who hope in the Lord*
> *Will renew their strength*
> *They will soar on wings like eagles*
> *They will run and not grow weary*
> *They will walk and not be faint."*
>   Isaiah 40:31